THE DIVINE OPENING

A HANDBOOK ON THE RULES AND ETIQUETTES OF THE TARIQA TIJANIYYA

Compiled By:
Muqaddam Anwar Ahmad Bayat Cisse (South Africa)
Ustadh Sa'ad Ngamdu (Nigeria)
Imam Fakhruddin Owaisi (USA)

Published in 2015 by
Fayda Books, Publishing & Distribution

ISBN 978-0-9913813-5-7

©2015 Atlanta Georgia, USA

No Part of This Book May Be Reproduced in Any Form Without Prior Permission from the Publishers. All Rights Reserved

Cover design by: Muhammadan Press

Table of Contents

Acknowledgement	7
Dedication	9
Letter to the Muslim Umma	11
Publishers Foreward	13
Biography of Imam Shaykh Tijani bin 'Ali Cissé	15
Introduction	17
Chapter 1: Biography of Shaykh Ahmad al-Tijani	21
Chapter 2: Conditions of the Tariqa Tijaniyya	27
Chapter 3: Obligatory Litanies (*Awrad*) of the Tariqa	33
Chapter 4: Ethics for Muqaddams and Murideen	49
Chapter 5: The Criticisms Against the Tariqa	65
Chapter 6: Bounties for the Sincere followers of Tariqa Tijaniyya	75
Chapter 7: The Position of Shaykh Ahmad al-Tijani	77
Chapter 8: Frequently Asked Questions (FAQs)	79
Glossary	

Acknowledgement

The authors would like to especially thank the following individuals for their guidance and assistance in creating this work: Imam Shaykh Tijani Cissé (Sénégal), Shaykh Mahi Cissé (Sénégal), Shaykh Baye Haiba (Mauritania), Ummi Mareldia Van Graan (South Africa), Dr. Abubakar Mulvane (South Africa), Sayyidah Najmirah Abdullah (South Africa), Sayyidah Zahra Sa'ad Abubakar (South Africa), Dr. Zachary Wright (USA), Ryan-Yusuf Hilliard (USA), Imam Hanif (USA), Fahmie Bassadien (South Africa), Muhammad Cissé (Liberia), Sidi Abdul Baqee (South Africa), Umm Sulayman (USA), 'Imran Solomons, Altaf Abdullah Fakie, Khalil Cathrada, 'Imran Sonday, and Abdul-Wurith Parker.

We ask Allah to shower all of the above mentioned, with abundant blessings and happiness in this life as well as the next. Amin.

Ma'Salaam,

Muqaddam Anwar Ahmad Bayat Cisse (South Africa)

Ustadh Sa'ad Ngamdu (Nigeria)

Imam Fakhruddin Owaisi (USA)

Dedication

Praise be to Allah (swt), This humble effort is dedicated to his Eminence, the Succor (Ghawth) of his Time, the true inheritor of Shaykh Ibrahim Niasse (ra), the symbol of Haqîqah and Shari'a, the Manifestation of Truth by the Truth and who has guided the world on the Straightest of Paths, a man who emulated the Prophet (saws) step by step, a complete 'arif, who fortified Islam in every Murid's heart, Shaykh Hassan 'Ali Cissé (ra), may Allah (swt) have a special mercy upon him, and may he be with whom he loves, and may Allah (swt) reward him bountifully for his contribution to the religion of Islam throughout the world and to mankind in general. Amin.

Not an atom existed, except that it felt the sorrowful, yet graceful departure of our dear father. There was not an eye of any Tijani adherent (murid) that did not shed a tear because of his departure. All the hearts of the Gnostics ('arifun) bled, in the wake of his departure. Each generation of human beings has its own expe- rience of sadness; and the sadness of the passing of Shaykh Hassan Cissé stands unmatched in our generation. Coming to terms with this painful reality was only by Allah's mercy and because of Shaykh Hassan's (ra) legacy. It seems as if Shaykh Hassan is alive because of the tremendous work he has left behind which is con- tinuously growing. Shaykh Hassan has taken the Fayda of Shaykh Ibrahim Niasse (ra) throughout the world, especially the English-speaking communities. There- fore, he is the father of the Fayda of the English-speaking world. Hence, this book is inspired by him, and may Allah (swt) reward him for that. We ask Allah (swt) to support all of Shaykh Hassan Cissé's inheritors to successfully continue with the mission of Shaykh Ibrahim Niasse (ra), which is nothing but the mission of our hero, our Prophet Muhammad (saws). The biography of Shaykh Hassan (ra) is found on the home page of the web site "Noor-ala-Noor" and the homepage of the African American Islamic Institute (AAII).

www.aaii.info

www.tijani.org

We appeal to every murid to recite eleven Surah al-Ikhlas and ten Salat al-Fatihi as a gift (hadiya) to Shaykh Hassan Cissé (ra).

Letter to the ummah

Dear Muslim brothers and sisters,

Oh Ummah of the Prophet Muhammad (saws)! We, the Murideen of the Chief Imam of the Grand Mosque of Medina Baye-Kaolack, Shaykh Tijani Cissé, humbly appeal to your kind-heartedness to constantly look after your Muslim brothers. They vigilantly seek to practice extra worship ('ibada) via the Tariqa Tijaniyya. When meeting them in your journey towards Allah (swt), encourage them to be constant in these spiritual practices. If by chance or destiny you have read this book, hold them to the criteria of the perfect murid and/or *muqaddam*. If you find them weak, advise them and remember all servants have faults.

Muqaddam Anwar Ahmad Bayat Cisse

Publishers' foreward

In the Name of Allah the Most Gracious, the Most Merciful,

May the prayer and peace of Allāh be upon the secret of the Divine Essence (*dhāt*), the light of the Divine Essence, our master Muhammad (saw), the light of existence (*wujūd*), the spiritual support (*madad*) of existence.

When I was asked by Imam Fakhruddin, to publish this book, I felt a deep honor and blessing from the Divine Presence, completely and immediately. I understood that this book contained the first published explanation, proof and defense of the Tarîqa Tijâniyya, written by the budding stars of Islam and Tarîqa, of my generation.

The amazing blessing, to have Fayda Books as an instrument to publish and disseminate this exposition of light, is overwhelming. We beseech Allah's Tawfiq and his permission to continue as a servant of the Holy Hadara.

May Allah Give Us Allah.

Ibrahim Ahmed Dimson
Publisher, Fayda Books

Biography of Imam Shaykh Tijani Cissé

Shaykh Tijani bin 'Ali Cissé (b. 1955) is the second son of Shaykh Ibrahim's most beloved Murid, Shaykh Sayyidi 'Ali Cissé (ra), and his first daughter, Fatima Zahra Niasse. After memorizing Qur'an in Medina-Baye Kaolack, Shaykh Tijani himself became a Qur'an teacher in Medina Baye while continuing his Islamic studies. In his late teens, he devoted himself full-time to personalized instruction (Majalis al-'Ilm), first under his father, Shaykh Sayyidi 'Ali Cissé (ra) (1971-1972); and then under his grandfather, Shaykh Ibrahim (1973). He was the last person to be instructed by Shaykh Ibrahim in the classical texts, focusing mostly on Arabic literature and poetry. He would later receive the highest of licenses from his father, Shaykh Sayyidi 'Ali Cissé, who told him: "Whatever Shaykh Ibrahim gave me, I am giving you."

After completing his early education in Sénégal, he traveled to Egypt where he lived with his elder brother, Shaykh Hassan Cissé (ra) during his last year of study in Cairo. Like his brother, Shaykh Tijani excelled in his formal studies in Egypt; the result, he says, of the rigor of the informal instruction given him in Sénégal. He graduated first in his class in the al-Azhar Preparatory School, receiving his diploma in Arabic language in 1974. He received his Baccalaureate in 1977 in Arabic Language, graduating fourth in his class. By 1981, he had distinguished himself at the University of al-Azhar with a degree in the Faculty of Theology ('usul al-din) department of Prophetic Traditions (hadith).

The Sénégalese government recognized the scholarship of Shaykh Tijani Cissé, and appointed him Sénégal's General Commissioner for the Hajj in 2001. In 2006, he was recognized yet again, by Sénégalese President, Abdoulaye Wade and appointed a Sénégalese "Special Missions Ambassador", a position he holds until the present time. He also received Sénégal's distinguished award, the Ordre National du Mérite in 1993. His country's high esteem for his scholarship was revealed most recently by a personal visit of President Abdoulaye Wade to the Shaykh's home in Medina Baye in 2008.[1]

---

1   Zachary Wright; http://tijani.org

The divine opening

The leading representatives of the legacy of Shaykh Ibrahim Niasse (ra) unanimously agreed upon the installation of Shaykh Tijani Cissé as Imam of the Grand Mosque of Medina Baye. His inauguration on August 15, 2008 was attended by delegations from Nigeria, Mauritania, Ghana, south America, China, Europe, Indonesia, Malaysia and the United States of America.

Shaykh Ibrahim's Last Will designated leadership of Medina Baye's Grand Mosque to his closest disciple, Shaykh Saydi Ali Cissé, then to be passed next to his eldest son, Shaykh Hassan, and thereafter "to whomever Allah (swt) wills." The unanimous validation of Shaykh Tijani Cissé as the community's new Imam proved him to be he "whom Allah (swt) wills" according to the will of Shaykh Ibrahim Niasse (ra). May Allah (swt) prolong his life, and allow his lofty aspiration (himma) to lift the hearts of those in need. The person accompanying Shaykh Tijani Cissé in this mission is his younger brother, Shaykh Mahy Cissé. He is an 'alim in his own right in Islamic studies, and has a Degree from al-Azhar University in Arabic literature, whom Shaykh Hassan has left the running of the Institute of all the Islamic sciences in Medina Baye to as well as the academy of 70 hifz schools in Medina Baye and the role of Imam of Kossi Atlanta. His biography is also available on the AAII web site's home page.

Introduction

All praise belongs to Allah (swt), who has put the source of His wisdom in His chosen ones amongst His creation. Peace and blessings be on our Master Muhammad (saws), the Opener and the Sealer of Prophets and Messengers, and the chosen one from the children of 'Abd al-Muttalib, son of Hashim. He is Divine Mercy, and the straightway of Allah (swt). May Allah (swt) bless His family, and may these blessings be according to his true position with Allah (swt) and His magnanimous value in our hearts. May Allah (swt) be pleased with our Shaykh, the Hidden Pole (*al-Qutb al-Maktum*), and raise us in his group. May Allah (swt) quench our thirst in Paradise from *al-Rahiq al-Makhtum* (a lake in paradise with an aroma of musk).

This book contains information about rules and conditions of the Tariqa and its litanies, and the ethics (*adab*) of the adherent (*murid*) with himself and his *Shaykh*. The book also highlights the spiritual blessings achieved by the murid, the spiritual position of the Shaykh and the position of *al-Qutb al-Maktum* (ra). The book also responds to criticisms facing the Tariqa Tijaniyya, and proves its practices with evidences from the Qur'an, the Sunna and the books of great Islamic scholars and jurists.

This book contains extracts of many Tijani books, such as: *Jawahir al-ma'ani* by Shaykh 'Ali Harazim al-Barada, *Kitab al-Rimah* by al-Hajj Umar Tal al-Futi, *Ahzab wa awrad* and *Qasd al-sabil* by Shaykh Muhammad al-Hafiz al-Misri, *al-Fat'h al-rabbani* by Shaykh Muhammad bin Hasanayn al-Tafsawi, *al-Futuhat al-rabbaniyya* by Shaykh Ahmad Shinqiti and *Ruh al-adab* by Shaykh Ibrahim Niasse and its translation, *"The Spirit of Good Morals"* by Shaykh Hassan 'Ali Cissé, as well as other works.

We compiled the book in this manner in order to help clear up misun- derstandings about the Tijani Tariqa. The book does not deal with Sufism in general, as it focuses specifically on Tariqa Tijaniyya only. If the reader has questions or criticisms with regards to subjects not discussed in this book, we advise them to research other great Sufi books like *Ihya 'ulum al-din* by Imam al-Ghazali, *al-Hikam*

The divine opening

by Shaykh Ibn 'Ata'illah al-Iskandari or *Shawahid al-haqq* by Shaykh Yusuf al-Nabhani.

Sufism (Tasawwuf) originates from the hadith narrated by Sayyidina 'Umar bin al-Khattab (ra) named "The Hadith of Jibril (al-Hadith al-Jibriliyya)":

> "One day we were sitting with Prophet Muhammad (saws) and a stranger came and sat with us, wearing a very white garment, having dark black hair, with no sign of travel on him and none of us knew him. He then sat in front of the Prophet (saws), his knees against the Prophets' knees and placed his hands on the Prophets' thighs. And he said, 'Oh Messenger of Allah! Tell me about Islam.' The Prophet (saws) replied, 'Islam is to bear witness that there is no god except Allah, and Muhammad is the Messenger of Allah, to perform Salah, to give Zakah, to fast the month of Ramadan and to perform Hajj if you are able to do so.' Thereafter the man said to the Prophet (saws), 'You have spoken the truth. Tell me about Iman.' The Prophet (saws) answered, 'Iman is to believe in Allah, His Angels, His books, His Messengers, the Day of Judgment and to believe in Destiny of good and evil." Again the man said, "You have spoken the truth. Please tell me about Ihsan." We were surprised at this person who was asking the Holy Prophet (saws) and thereafter saying the answers are correct. Thereafter the Prophet (saws) answered regarding Ihsan, and said, "Ihsan is to worship Allah as if you are seeing Him; and if you do not see Him, indeed He sees you." After asking other questions regarding the Day of Judgment and its signs the man departed. And the Prophet (saws) asked his Companions, "Do you know who the questioner was?" The Companions replied, "No, Allah and His Messenger know best." The Prophet (saws) said, "He was Jibril (as) who came to teach you your religion."

By observing the *hadith* we find that the *'Ulama'* has extracted the three core subjects that Islam is comprised of, e.g. jurisprudence (*fiqh*), Divine Unity (*tawhid*) and spiritual purification (*tazkiyya* and *tasawwuf*). **Islam** comprises of bearing witness that there is no god but Allah (swt) and that Prophet Muhammad (saws) is His Messenger; conditions, beautifications and nullifications of prayer (*Salat*); rules guiding alms (zakat), and the correct performance of the Pilgrimage (Hajj), and the rules of fasting (*sawm*). This comprehensive subject is called jurisprudence (*'usul al-fiqh*).

Secondly, **Iman** comprises of believing in Allah (swt), His Essence and His Attributes, His Angels, His Books, His Messengers, the Day of Resurrection and Judgment, and destiny of good and evil. This subject matter is called and compiled as Divine Unity ('ilm al-tawhid).

Thirdly, **Ihsan** comprises of worshiping Allah (swt) as if you are seeing Him. The method of achieving this beautiful spiritual condition is a subject named and compiled as (*Tasawwuf*). This subject, since the demise of the Prophet (saws), has been presented to the world by numerous shuyukh through spiritual Paths (*Tariqa*). There are many Paths, such as the *Tijaniyya, Qadiriyya, Naqshbandiyya, Chistiyya,* and *Shadhiliyya,* which all lead to the state of Ihsan. Although there has been an arrival of many distortions, none of the great 'Ulama' have neglected the importance of this subject, which has constantly been shown to us in the Holy Qur'an:

"By the sun, and its brightness; and the moon, as she follows him, by the day, which shows its splendor; by the night which draws a veil over it; by the heaven and Him Who made it; by the earth and Him Who spread it; by the soul and Him Who perfected it; and inspired it with knowledge of what is wrong for it and what is right for it; indeed successful will be the one who keeps it pure, and indeed (a) failure will be the one who corrupts it!"

[Qur'an 91:1-10]

In these verses above, Allah (swt) swears by different elements of His creation to emphasize the importance of purifying the ego-self (*nafs*). In the last two verses, after Allah (swt) has been swearing by His elements, He says that whoever has purified oneself has succeeded and whoever has not purified himself has lost a great deal.

Always remember that most distortions found in this subject are due to a lack of research by some scholars as well as a lack of knowledge of the science of *tasawwuf*, either by seekers or non-seekers. Consequently, Imam Malik bin Anas (ra) says:

"Whoever acts on the Law (Shari'a) without knowing its Reality (Haqiqa) is a degenerate; and whoever acts on Haqiqa without Shari'a is an infidel. Only the one who combines the two into balanced practice proves true."

In this century, we have the *Tariqa Tijaniyya*, which is the latest of all the other *turuq*. Some Tijani elders have said that there have been three hundred and thirteen different *turuq* that have come to the *Ummah* of the Prophet (saws) in order to revive Islam. Each *Tariqa* representing one of the Companions (as'hab) that fought alongside the Prophet (saws) in the Battle of Badr and this *Tariqa Tijaniyya* is the three-hundred and thirteenth one, known as *al-Tariqa al-Khatm* (the Seal of Paths).

We introduce this Tariqa to you by the story of the great Egyptian *Shaykh* Muhammad bin 'Abd-Allah bin Hasanayn al-Tafsawi (ra), the author of *al-Fat'h al-Rabba- ni*, on how he entered this *Tariqa* as he narrated it to us in his book. He was born into an honorable *Naqshabandi* community, in his village resided only ten people from the *Tariqa Tijaniyya*. Whenever he heard the recital of the *tijânî*

Wazifa, his heart would be touched. However, his father was not keen on him becoming a *Tijani*. One day, after traveling to Cairo, he had a dream of Shaykh 'Umar Tal al-Futi (ra), the great West African shaykh and author of *al-Rimah*. The Shaykh was in a big congregation close to the mosque of his village. Sidi Tafsawi then recited Surah Ya Sin in the *Warsh* dialect, in front of Shaykh 'Umar al-Futi while sitting. The Shaykh was excited and asked him if he had memorized the Qur'an. He replied that he had memorized the Holy Qur'an in *Hafs* and *Warsh* dialectic styles, he thereafter ate some meat with Shaykh 'Umar, and then woke up. He had this dream when he was only seventeen years of age. Sidi al-Tafsawi then dreamt two nights later that he was with a Tijani of his village in al-Goria Street (where the main Tijani *Zawiya* in Cairo is situated), where he met a *muqaddam* who addressed him as Shaykh Muhammad, and he immediately requested initiation into the *Tariqa Tijaniyya* from that muqaddam, and received it. Three days later, he had another dream and he saw himself in the mosque of his village, he performed full ablution and entered the mosque were he saw Sidi al-Bashir al-Zaytuni (ra) and requested the Tariqa from him.

Later when he travelled to Cairo with his father, they visited the tomb of Imam Husayn (ra), grandson of the Prophet (saws). When entering the tomb to make ziyara (visit), he asked his father to permit him to take the Tariqa Tijaniyya with Imam Husayn (ra) as the mediator between them, and his father agreed. Thereafter, he took the Tariqa, and later became a great shaykh and muqaddam.

We have related this story in order to highlight the link between Allah (swt) and His servants. Allah (swt) is The One who has guided this shaykh to the Tariqa Tijaniyya. There is no competition between Tariqa Tijaniyya and other paths. The path that Allah (swt) has presented you to approach Him is undeniably His decision. Therefore, we advise the followers of other paths to love their shuyukh and their litanies (*awrad*), because all authentic paths lead to Allah (swt).

CHAPTER
One

Biography of Shaykh Ahmad al-Tijani (ra)

Sidi Abul-Abbas Ahmad al-Tijani was born in the Southwest Algerian oasis town of Ain Madi on the twelfth of *Safar* in the year 1150 (1737 C.E.). He was a descendant of the Prophet Muhammad (saws) through Fatima Zahra's first son Hassan and later through Mawlay Idris, the celebrated founder of Morocco. His father was Sidi Muhammad b. al-Mukhtar b. Ahmad b. Muhammad b. Salam, a prominent scholar whose family hailed from the Moroccan Abda tribe and whose grandfather had immigrated to Ain Madi fleeing a Portuguese invasion less than a century before Shaykh Tijani's birth. This same ancestor was perhaps one of the more renowned of the Tijani line prior to Shaykh Ahmad Tijani, and it is reported that he used to engage so much in spiritual retreat (*khalwa*) that he would have to walk to the five prayers in the mosque with his face covered, otherwise onlookers would fall so heedlessly in love with him that they would thereafter never be able to separate from him. Shaykh Tijani's mother, Aisha, was the daughter of Muhammad b. Sanusi (no known relation to Muhammad al-Sanusi, the founder of the *Sanusiyya*), and was noted for her piety and generosity.[2]

The young Shaykh Tijani continued in the scholarly tradition of his family and city, memorizing the Qur'an by the age of seven, then turning to the study of jurisprudence (*fiqh and usul al-fiqh*), Prophetic traditions (*Hadith*), explanation of the Qur'an (*tafsir*), Qur'anic recitation (*tajwid*), grammar (*nahw*) and literature (*adab*), among other branches of the traditional Islamic sciences. According to the *Jawahir*, the Shaykh mastered all of these fields at a very young age, in part due to the force of his resolve but also because of the quality of his teachers. Among his first instructors were masters of their fields, such as Sidi Mabruk Ibn Ba'afiyya Mi-dawi al-Tijani (not mentioned in the *Jawahir* as being a relation to Ahmad Tijani),

---

2 *al-Fat'h al-rabbani*

The divine opening

with whom he studied the Mukhtasar of Sidi Khalil, the *Risala* and the *Muqaddama* of Ibn Rushd (Averoes) and the *Kitab al-'Ibada* of al-Akhdari.

Shaykh Tijani's prodigious capacity for learning at such an early age is explained in the *Jawahir* by the Shaykh's own statement: *"When I begin something, I never turn from it."* In another passage describing his love for the people of religion, the *Jawahir* describes him as a youth of powerful intelligence, such that nothing escaped his realization. Thus it was that even after he had mastered the sciences available in Ain Madi and had become, by the age of twenty, according to the *Jawahir*, a great scholar, jurist and man of letters such that people were coming to partake of the knowledge of this newest *Mufti* (a scholar licensed to issue legal decisions), his thirst for more knowledge pushed him to leave the city of his birth in 1171/1758.

The obvious destination for any seeker of Islamic knowledge in the Maghrebi context was Fas Morocco, the long-established political, intellectual, cultural and religious capital of the area. According to the *Jawahir*, the young Shaykh Tijani spent his time in Fas studying Hadith and generally seeking out the people of piety and religion. Among his teachers in Fas were many famous for their knowledge and saintliness. Their names are provided here to demonstrate Shaykh Ahmad Tijani's contact with some of the more significant luminaries of eighteenth-century Moroccan Sufism. Al-Tayyib b. Muhammad al-Sharif of Wazan (d. 1180/1767), who was head of the *Wazzaniyya* Sufi order at the time and the student of the famous Shaykh Tuhami descending from the *Jazuli* shaykh Ahmad al-Sarsari, gave Tijani permission to give spiritual instruction, only to have the young scholar refuse so that he might work harder on himself before becoming a spiritual guide. Sidi Abdullah b. 'Arabi al-Mada'u (d. 1188) was likewise impressed with his student, telling him that God was guiding him by the hand, and before Tijani left him, the old scholar washed his student with his own hands. Another scholar to predict to Tijani an exalted spiritual attainment was Sidi Ahmad al-Tawash (d. 1204). From Sidi Ahmad al-Yemeni, Shaykh Tijani took the *Qadariyya* Sufi order, and from Abu Abdullah Sidi Muhammad al-Tizani he took the *Nasiriyya* order. He also took the order of Abu Abbas Ahmad al-Habib al-Sijilmasy (d. 1165), who came to him in a dream, put his mouth on his, and taught him a secret name. Although Tijani did receive spiritual permission (*idhn*) in these orders, his association with them should not be considered the essential element in his spiritual development. But the imprint of his early affiliation with these orders was not completely lost with the later development of the Tijaniyya, and their emphasis on an elite "orthodox" Sufism, firmly rooted within the bounds of the Qur'an and Sunna, was an essential component of Shaykh Tijani's new order, as will be seen later in chapter three.

Even from the time of Shaykh Tijani's first visit to Fas, the young scholar's ascendant motivation seemed to be the attainment of a spiritual opening (*fath*). So when another of his teachers, Sidi Muhammad al-Wanjili (d. 1185), a man known for his saintliness, predicted for him a *maqaam* (spiritual station) of *Qutbaniyya* (Polehood) similar to that of Abu Hasan al-Shadhili, but that his spiritual opening (*fath*) would come in the desert, Tijani hastened his departure from Fas. The Jawahir reports that he spent some time in the desert Zawiya of the famous Qutb Sidi Abd al-Qadir b. Muhammad al-Abyad (known as Sidi al-Shaykh) before returning to Ain Madi, only to leave his home soon again to return to al-Abyad before moving on to Tlemcen. His activities during this time consisted of teaching Qur'anic exegesis (*tafsir*) and Hadith in whatever town he happened to be staying while continuing an apparently rigorous practice of asceticism, including frequent fasting and supererogatory worship. During his stay in Tlemcen, he received, through Divine inspiration, greater assurance of his coming grand illumination.

It was from southwest Algeria, then, that Shaykh Ahmad Tijani set out in 1186/1773 to accomplish the requisite Islamic pilgrimage (*Hajj*). Shaykh Tijani's first stop of note enroute to Mecca was at Algiers, where he met Sidi Muhammad b. Abd al-Rahman al-Azhary (d. 1793), a prominent *muqaddam* (spiritual guide) of the Khalwatiyya Sufi order who had received initiation at the hands of Shaykh al-Azhar Muhammad al-Hifni. The Khalwatiyya (Helveti), originating in fourteenth century Anatolia, had become by the eighteenth century, under the tutelage of Mustafa al-Bakri, one of the most prominent orders in Egypt and a locus for Islamic and Sufi renewal.

Shaykh Tijani's affiliation with this order was perhaps the most significant influence on his thought, prior to his waking meetings with the Prophet, and he did not leave Algiers before receiving initiation at the hands of al-Azhary. No doubt, such an encounter would have provided additional impetus to meet, as he later would, some of the day's most renowned Khalwati scholars, such as Mahmud al-Kurdi and Muhammad al-Samman, while passing through Egypt and the Hijaz.

Shaykh Ahmad Tijani's journey East brought him also to Tunis, home of the famous Zaytuna mosque and university, which predates both the Azhar in Cairo and the Qarawin in Fas. Indicative of the ease with which foreign scholars could integrate into diverse Islamic communities, upon his entry into Tunis, Shaykh Tijani immediately met with the people of saintly renown, such as Sidi Abd al-Samad al-Rahwi, and took up teaching at Zaytuna, this time his syllabus included Ibn 'Atta Allah's *Kitab al-hikam*. It seems he made enough of an impression on the scholars there, that the Emir, Bey Ali (r. 1757-1782), offered him a lucrative permanent teaching position at Zaytuna. However, the Emir's request had the opposite effect on Shaykh Tijani to that which was hoped for and, reportedly not wanting to accept dependence on state authority, he continued his journey east.

The divine opening

Arriving in Mecca just after Ramadan in the year 1187/1774, Shaykh Ahmad Tijani stayed long enough to accomplish the rites of the *Hajj*. During his stay there he also, as was his custom, sought out the people of "goodness, piety, righteousness and happiness." His search led him to a mysterious saint from India, Ahmad b. Abdullah al-Hindi, who had made a vow to speak to no one except his servant. On knowledge of Tijani's presence at his house, al-Hindi sent him the message, "You are the inheritor of my knowledge, secrets, gifts and lights," and informed the pilgrim that he himself was to die in a matter of days (it came to pass on the exact day al-Hindi had predicted for himself), but that he should go visit the *Qutb* (Pole) Muhammad al-Samman when in Medina.

After accomplishing the *ziyara* (visitation) to the Prophet's tomb, where "God completed his aspiration and longing" to greet the Prophet, Shaykh Tijani went to visit the renowned Shaykh Muhammad Abd al-Karim al-Samman (d. 1189/1775). Like al-Kurdi, al-Samman was a member of the Khalwatiyya order, being one of two students given full *ijaza* (permission) by Mustafa al-Bakri; the other was al-Kurdi's shaykh, Muhammad al-Hifni. Aside from his own intellectual and spiritual prowess, al-Samman has become famous because of another disciple, Ahmad al-Tayyib (d. 1824), who spread his ideas in the Sudan as the Sammaniyya order. Before Shaykh Tijani's departure, al-Samman informed him of certain secret "names" and told him that he was to be the *al-qutb al-jami'* (the comprehensive Pole). On his return from the Hijaz, Shaykh Tijani stopped in Cairo and visited Mahmud al-Kurdi, the Khalwati representative in Egypt whom he had first visited on his way to the Hijaz. The *Jawahir* reports that many of the *'ulama* of the city came to visit the travelling scholar during this second visit. Demonstrating his profound respect for his teachers of the Khalwati tradition, Tijani accepted from al-Kurdi to be a *muqaddam* (propagator) of the Khalwati order in North Africa. Although Tijani's later initiation at the hands of the Prophet would obviate its need, the *Jawahir* reproduces the chain of transmission (*silsilah*) of the Khalwatiyya, stretching from the Prophet through Ali ibn Abi Talib, Hasan al-Basri, Junayd, Umar al-Khalwati (from whom the order derives its name), Bakri, and Kurdi (not to mention all the names) to Shaykh Tijani.

The beginning of a distinctive "Tijani" order can be located with the appearance of the Prophet Muhammad to Shaykh Ahmad Tijani in a waking vision. This occurred in 1784, in the desert oasis of Abi Samghun. The Prophet informed him that he himself was his initiator on the Path and told him to leave the shaykhs he had previously followed. The Shaykh then received the basis of a new *wird* and was given permission to give "spiritual training to the creation in [both] the general and unlimited (*itlaq*)." The Prophet told him: *"You are not indebted for any favor from the shaykhs of the Path, for I am your means (wasita) and your support in the [spiritual] realization, so leave the entirety of what you have taken from all the tariqas."*

Shaykh Ahmad Tijani and a group of his closest companions took up residence in Fas beginning in 1213/1798. By the time of his arrival in Fas, Shaykh Tijani's fame as a scholar possessing religious charisma or blessing (*baraka*) had spread throughout the Maghreb, so that his entry into the city was a matter of some importance for the political and religious establishment. The Shaykh was met by a delegation of scholars selected by the Sultan. The relationship that developed between Shaykh Tijani and Sultan Mawlay Sulayman is important in understanding the religious personality of both men. After a series of tests to ascertain the veracity of Tijani's claims to sainthood, such as giving the saint money in a manner he would not have been able to accept as a man of religion, Mawlay Sulayman became closely linked to the newcomer, appointing him to his council of religious scholars and giving him a large house ("the House of Mirrors"). The Sultan's initiation into the Tijaniyya has often been denied by non-Tijanis, but Tijanis have maintained his discipleship to their Shaykh. Tijani tradition has chronicled a series of letters between Shaykh Tijani and the Sultan clearly indicating a shaykh-disciple relationship. In one exchange, the Shaykh writes the Sultan urging him to fear God and keep to His command and then informs him of the some of the benefits of the Tijani *wird* as told to him by the Prophet, and tells him of the proper manners for experiencing the vision of the Prophet. The Sultan replied,

> "The ransom of our parents, our master and our shaykh and our Muhammadan example, Abul-'Abbas Sidi Ahmad. I praise God to you and to Him and I send blessings and peace upon His noble Prophet. Your most blessed lines have reached us, and we praise God the Most High on account of what He has made special for us by them from the pleasure of the master, the Messenger of God ... and this matter I do not want that I should allow myself to leave its performance, and I am not safe from losing or neglecting its fulfillment ... [and I pray that you] remove me from all that prevents me from looking at his [the Prophet's] noble face, that [you may] surround me with the degree of those close to the glory of the Messenger of God. And [this] is needed of you, since you know that my righteousness is a righteousness from my guardianship of God over them [the people], and that my corruption is their corruption, so the prayer for me is a prayer for the general [population]."

Aside from whatever esoteric connection existed between the Sultan and the founder of the Tijaniyya, another explanation of Mawlay Sulayman's warm reception of Shaykh Ahmad was the fact that the Sultan "found, in the person of Shaykh Tijani, the symbol that personified, by his behavior and his teaching, the indelible precepts of the *Shari'a*." Certainly, the Shaykh's situation of Sufism firmly within Islamic sacred law, while maintaining the ascendancy of the *Tariqa Muhammadiyya*, the "path of the Prophet," over both Sufi and *Fiqh* (jurisprudence) historical traditions, would have been attractive to the reform-minded Sultan.

The Shaykh's time in Fas was largely occupied with the solidification of the *tariqa* and the training and sending out of *muqaddams* (propagators). Before the end of his life, he had attracted thousands of followers and sent out *muqaddams* such as Ali Harazem Barada, Muhammad al-Ghali and Muhammad al-Hafiz as far away as the Hijaz and Mauritania. Before the completion of the Tijani zawiya, his followers met at the Shaykh's own house, the House of Mirrors. This house can still be visited today, and although it has fallen into a state of disrepair, its original majesty has not been lost. It has an expansive courtyard decorated entirely with blue and yellow *zellij* tile work with a large fountain in the middle, flanked by a number of rooms that include what was the Shaykh's library, a room for *khalwa* (spiritual retreat), a salon, the bedroom, the kitchen, etc., with rooms for the Shaykh's family and guests on the second floor. It is easy to imagine the house serving as the center of prayer and for the teaching and diffusion of the Shaykh's ideas.

Established in *Fas*, the Shaykh's following continued to grow, prompting him in 1215 (1800), by order of the Prophet, to begin construction of the Tijani zawiyya that still serves as a place of congregation for the order to this day. The construction of this fabulous specimen of Moroccan artistry was financed by Tijani's followers as well as from his own funds. Shaykh Ahmad Tijani passed from this world in 1230 (1815) at the age of eighty. He left behind, a firmly established order, the *Tariqa Muhammadiyya* emphasis of which inspired many of his later followers to renew and spread Islam in diverse communities far from the mother zawiya in Fas. Shaykh Ahmad Tijani is buried in his *zawiya* in *Fas*, which today remains a center of congregation for Tijanis around the world.

CHAPTER Two

The Conditions of the Tariqa Tijaniyya:

1. To receive initiation into the Tariqa from a qualified and licensed Muqaddam.[3]
2. The person taking the Tariqa cannot have any other Tariqa or s/he should give up what s/he had before.
3. The person cannot visit non-Tijani saints (Awliya'), alive or dead, for the purpose of deriving spiritual benefit.

Once, Shaykh Ahmad al-Tijani (ra) was ordered, by the Prophet (saws) to remove his permission to perform the Tijani litany (ijaza) from two Murideen who visited a great shaykh named Shaykh 'Abd al-Salam bin Mashish (ra), the owner of Salat al-Mashishiyya. The Prophet (saws) also said to Shaykh Ahmad al-Tijani (ra) that there is an issue that many shuyukh have disregarded (i.e. whoever gives allegiance [bay'ah] to one shaykh and visited another, with the intention of deriving spiritual benefits, cannot benefit from either of them). The Prophet (saws) also said that the Tijani Murideen may visit his Companions (ra).

Shaykh Ahmad al-Tijani (ra) said that three things will cut the Murid from us (the fold of the Tariqa Tijaniyya): (1) taking another Tariqa having already taken this one, (2) visiting non-Tijani saints, alive or dead, for spiritual benefit, and (3) abandoning the litany (*Wird, Wazifa & Dhirk-Jumuah*).

Shaykh al-Shinqiti, a great Tijani shaykh of Mauritania, said, "Visiting your Shaykh is very important in this Tariqa." He quotes from *Mukhtasar Khalil* (a Maliki jurisprudence treatise) that if someone starts observing supererogatory duties (*nawafil*), fasting or praying, he cannot break it except by the word of his parents

---

3   *al-Futuhat al-rabbaniyya*

or shaykh. This fiqh point clearly illustrates how Islam regards the shuyukh. It also teaches the Murid that s/he should constantly visit his shaykh, even by telephone, because this action beautifies and completes him in the Tariqa.

Shaykh al-Shinqiti also added that the Tijani Murid should respect all saints from other Paths, because respecting them is respecting the Prophet (saws). Special attention and manners (*adab*) should be given to his (saws) descendants (*ashraf*). Thus, the Tijani Murid should not think that because he cannot benefit from them spiritually that they are not great in the sight of Allah (swt), for truly, they are our masters and people of great position in the sight of Allah (swt), and they are our heroes in establishing the religion of Allah (swt). However, at this time Allah (swt) has blessed the Tijani Murid s o m u c h , that if he recites *Jawharat al-Kamal* twelve times, with the intention of visitation (*ziyara*), he will receive the reward of a person who has visited the Prophet (saws) at his tomb and all the previous Prophets and Messengers, as well as the Saintly Poles (Aqtab) and great saints (*awliya'*). More information about the *Jawharat al-Kamal* will be given later.

4. **To perform the ritual prayers (Salat) in congregation as much as possible.**

Shaykh Ahmad al-Tijani (ra) placed much emphasis on this. He warned his aspirants from following Imams who do not complete their *ruku'* and *sajda* properly, explaining that a Muslim should relax in his *ruku'* and *sajda* to the extent that s/he should be able to recite three times with comfort::

"*Subhana Rabbi al-'Azim wa bi-hamdihi,*"

(سبحان ربي العظيم وبحمده)

"*Subhana Rabbi al-A'la wa bi-hamdihi,*"

(سبحان ربي الأعلى وبحمده)

And he (ra) went further in saying that holistic concentration (Khushu'a) is a condition of prayer, without it there is no prayer. Moreover, if the Imam does not have that concentration therein, both external and internal, the prayer is void as well as the prayer of those following him. Therefore, Murideen are advised not to continue following such an Imam. He (ra) added that if the Murid wants an excellent pious prayer, he should recite the aforementioned 10 times each in the *ruku'* and *sajdah* respectively.

5. **You should love your shaykh throughout your life.**

The Conditions of the Tariqa Tijaniyya:

6. **Don't feel satisfied with your worship ('ibada), or feel safe because you found yourself in a high spiritual position.**

Allah (swt) says in a *hadith qudsi*, "Don't feel safe even if you find yourself inside Paradise. Know that your father Adam (as) was inside Paradise and I took him out." What does that say about us, mere servants? Allah (swt) says, *"Do these people feel secure from Allah's scheme? But no one can feel secure from Allah's scheme except those who are already lost"*

(أفأمنوا مكر الله فلا يأمن مكر الله إلا القوم الخاسرون)

7. **You should not curse Shaykh Ahmad al-Tijani (ra) or be angry with him, or have hatred for him, or take him as an enemy.**

8. **When one takes this Tariqa Tijaniyya, s/he must adhere to it completely until death.**

9. **To believe that Shaykh Ahmad al-Tijani (ra) saw the Prophet (saws) in broad daylight.**

10. **Attend the Wazifa and Dhikr al-Jumu'ah in congregation.**

11. **To recite the "Jewel of Perfection" (Jawharat al-Kamal) with ablution and in a clean location.**

The Prophet (saws) and his four Rightly-Guided Successors (*Khulafa' al-Rashidun*) are in attendance of the *Wazifa*. Thus whoever recites *Jawharat al-Kamal* in or outside *Wazifa* after the seventh number has the honor of the attendance of the Prophet Muhammad (saws) and his four *Khulafa'* (ra) until the end, if Allah so wills. Therefore, it is good to place a clean, white sheet inside the circle or even if he is alone. However, there is no obligation in that.

The story of spreading the white sheet came about as related to us by Shaykh 'Abd al-Wahhab bin Taudi (ra), one of the special associates of Shaykh al-Tijani (ra). He says during the first *Wazifa*, which was being performed at the entrance of the home of Shaykh al-Tijani (ra), at that time, no mosque or *Zawiya* had been established yet. Therefore, for cleanliness and reverence of the attendance of the Prophet (saws), Shaykh al-Tijani (ra) requested a clean, white sheet for the *Wazifa*. Then later on the practice continued in the *Zawiya* and Shaykh al-Tijani (ra) never stopped or said anything regarding it. The author of *al-Jaysh al-Kabir* is quoted to have said that Shaykh Ahmad al-Tijani (ra) did not spread the white sheet during his lifetime, but it came about after his life as a beautification for *Wazifa*. However, Shaykh 'Abd al-Wahab bin Taudi's version has proven to be the most acceptable one, by virtue of his closer proximity and association to the Shaykh (ra) in comparison to the other.

12. The Murid should not boycott other Muslims, especially his Tijani brothers.
13. Don't be negligent in the regular recitation of the Tijani litany (Wird) by delaying it without good excuse.
14. Don't claim to be a saint (Wali) or authority (muqaddam) without authentic permission. This will lead the claimer to a bad ending as quoted from Jawahir al-ma'ani.
15. Respecting all the followers of Shaykh Ahmad al-Tijani (ra), more specifically the Special Ones. Shaykh Ahmad al-Tijani (ra) has said that the Murid should know that we have a very special position with Allah to the extent that mentioning it is forbidden (haram). This position is far beyond that which has been revealed to them; and if I was to reveal it, the true people of knowledge will be the first to judge me with disbelief (kufr). The least I can reveal is that whoever disrespects a Tijani, he could cause Allah to remove from them the good spiritual state that they find themselves in.
16. The Prophet (saws) said to Shaykh Ahmad al-Tijani (ra), "Tell your followers not to hurt me by hurting each other."
17. Facing the Qibla whenever possible during the recitation of the Wird, except for the traveler.
18. Reciting the Wird while seated, not lying down, reclining or standing unless you have a physical disposition that causes difficulty.
19. To always be virtuous and kind towards your parents. Shaykh al-Tijani (ra) said he who is not virtuous to his parents has failed in his journey in this Tariqa.
20. Avoid association of those who show enmity, hatred or displeasure with Shaykh Ahmad al-Tijani (ra).
21. If possible, picture your shaykh murabbi while reciting the Wird and likewise his shaykh. But if you can picture the Prophet (saws), that is better for concentration.

22. Sit with humility and piety as if the Prophet (saws) is sitting with you.
23. Always try to reflect on the meaning of the Wird. If you don't understand the words, try to listen to them attentively.
24. The Wird and Wazifa can only be interrupted by one's parents, shaykh and/or husband. Interruption in this context means, the Murid may show sign language to the matter at hand or may speak very briefly.
25. Whenever the Wird is to commence, the Murid must make his intention first. Example: morning or evening Wird and Wazifa. Intention is known as the worship of the heart, while the action is the worship of the limbs.
26. Whoever recites Jawharat al-Kamal seven times before going to bed, and has clean bed sheets, he will dream of Prophet (saws).
27. Whoever recites Jawharat al-Kamal daily will not die except as a great saint (Wali).
28. Do not eat and drink during the recitation of your Wird, not even a little.

*****

For more information on ethics of the Tariqa Tijaniyya, readers are advised to read **Ruh al-adab**, a book written by Shaykh Ibrahim Niasse (ra) at the age of 20 and translated into English by his grandson, Shaykh Hassan Cissé (ra). This book teaches how to be the best Murid and climb the highest stations, with Allah's permission.

*****

CHAPTER Three

Obligatory Litanies (awrad) of the Tariqa Tijaniyya

Allah says: "*Remember Me and I will remember you; thank Me and do not be ungrateful.*" (Qur'an 2:152)

"فاذكروني أذكركم واشكروا لي ولا تكفرون"

Shaykh Muhammad al-Hafiz al-Misri (ra)[4] said about this ayah that we should be cognizant that Allah (swt) has remembered us before we have the ability to remember Him. Therefore, we are already in debt in the remembrance of Allah (swt). In addition, the best of remembrances is reciting the Qur'an. Shaykh Ahmad al-Tijani (ra) encouraged the Murid in the recital of Qur'an and advises them to read at least one-thirtieth (*juz'*) a day, which equals to one completion of the Holy Qur'an every month. The best words in the Qur'an are "*La ilaha illa Allah*". And Prophet (saws) has also said that "the best of dhikr is *la ilaha illa Allah* ," narrated by Jabir (ra) (recorded by al-Nasa'i & hakim):

"أفضل الذكر لا إله إلا الله"

Therefore, it is understood that "*La ilaha illa Allah*" is the best of Qur'an and the best of *adhkar*, and this is the foundation of all *turuq*.

The blessed litany (Wird) of Shaykh Ahmad al-Tijani (ra) is of two types[5]: the obligatory *Wird*, also called *al-Lazim*, and supererogatory Wird. We will only be-

---

4   Ahzab wa awrad
5   al-Futuhat al-rabbaniyya

The divine opening

discussing the obligatory *Wird* in this book. The Wird *al-Lazim* consists of morning and evening *dhikr* and the *Wazifa*.

Morning and Evening *Wird*:

It is built on three Pillars: seeking Allah's (*swt*) forgiveness (*istighfar*), sending salutation of mercy and blessings (*salawat*) upon the Prophet (saws) by means of *Salat al-Fatihi*, and declaring the Divine Unity of Allah (*tahlil*).

The first pillar of the Tijani Wird is to say "*astaghfiru'llah*" 100 times.

(أستغفر الله)

O Allah ! I seek your forgiveness.

The *Murid* should be imagining Allah (swt) conveying him out of darkness.

The wisdom of the sequence starting with *istighfar* is to purify the heart from all impurity and darkness, and to place the *Murid* in a position of good comportment (*adab*). Thereafter, the recital of the salawat on the Prophet (saws) is to make him your intercessor in the presence of Allah (swt). As the greatest servant of Allah (swt) and the source of guidance for the whole Universe, the *salawat* establishes the love of the Prophet (saws) in the *Murid's* heart. Thereafter, the *Murid* recites the tahlil (*la ilaha illa Allah*) and enters the presence of Allah (swt).[6]

As for the bounties of seeking Allah's forgiveness, Allah (swt) says:

"وقلت استغفروا ربكم إنه كان غفارا *يرسل السماء عليكم مدرارا* ويمددكم بأموال وبنين ويجعل لكم جنات ويجعل لكم أنهارا* ما لكم لا ترجون لله وقارا"

"*And I said: seek forgiveness of your Lord, He is ever ready to forgive you, He will let loose the sky for you in plenteous rain and will help you with wealth and sons, and provide you gardens and flowing rivers. What is the matter with you that you do not regard the greatness of Allah .*" (Qur'an 71:10-14)

After reciting the *istighfar*,[7] the next pillar of the Tijani Wird is the salawat on the Prophet (saws), repeated 100 times. Any format is acceptable, but *Salat al-Fatih* is preferred in our Tariqah.

---

6   *Ahzab wa awrad*
7   *al-Futuhat al-rabbaniyya*

The *Murid* shall always remember that the Prophet (saws) is his intercessor in the presence of Allah (swt) and hold him with the highest reverence in his heart.

The Qur'an says regarding this:

"وما أرسلنا من رسول إلا ليطاع بإذن الله ولو أنهم إذ ظلموا أنفسهم جاءوك فاستغفروا الله واستغفر لهم الرسول لوجدوا الله توابا رحيما"

"We did not send any Messenger but to be obeyed in accordance with the will of Allah. Had they only come to you, when they had wronged themselves and asked Allah's forgiveness and the messenger had asked forgiveness for them, they would have found Allah Forgiving, Merciful". (Qur'an 4:64)

Allah said in the Holy Qur'an:

" إن الله وملائكته يصلون على النبي يأيها الذين آمنوا صلوا عليه وسلموا تسليما"

"Indeed Allah and His angels send blessings on the Prophet, O believers! Send your blessings on him and salute him with all respect". (Qur'an 33:56)

The Prophet (saws) was reported by al-Bukhari to have said:

فقد ثبت في الصحيح عنه صلى الله عليه وسلم انه قال:
لا يؤمن أحدكم حتى أكون أحب إليه من والده وولده والناس أجمعين.
فقال له عمر: يا رسول الله لأنت أحب إلي من كل شيء إلا من نفسي.
فقال النبي صلى الله عليه وسلم: لا والذي نفسي بيده حتى أكون أحب إليك من نفسك.
فقال له عمر: فإنه الآن والله لأنت أحب إلي من نفسي.
فقال النبي صلى الله عليه وسلم: الآن يا عمر!
و قد قال تعالى في الآية: النبي أولى بالمؤمنين من انفسهم

The divine opening

"I swear by The One in whose hand my life is! No one has complete faith until he loves me more than himself, his wealth, his children, and everybody else". Also in al-Bukhari, Sayyidina 'Umar (ra) said: "O the Messenger of Allah! I love you more than everything else except myself" and the Prophet (saws) said: "Not yet 'Umar! Until you love me more than yourself." Then 'Umar said: "O Messenger of Allah! I swear by Allah that I love you more than everything, including myself!" And the Prophet (saws) then said: "O 'Umar! Now you are complete."

And Allah (swt) said: *"The Prophet is closer to the believers than their own selves."* (Qur'an 33:6)

The Prophet (saws) also said:

"أنت مع من أحببت"

"You are with whom you love".

*****

Salat al-Fatih:[8]

اللهم صلِّ على سيدنا محمد الفاتح لما أُغلق والخاتم لما سبق

ناصر الحق بالحق والهادي إلى الصراط المستقيم

و على آله حق قدره و مقداره العظيم

Meaning;

"Oh Allah! Praise with peace our Master Muhammad, the One who has opened that which was closed, and sealed that which has passed, the Supporter of the truth with the truth, and the Guide to your straightway. And bless his family. And these blessings may it be according to his true position with you and his magnanimous value."

And as for the bounteous reward of it, our Shaykh has informed us that one day he asked the Master of existence, Muhammad (saws) regarding its rewards. He was informed that reciting it once equals six thousand times all the glorifications, all the remembrances, and all supplications, big and small recited in the world. Shaykh al-Tijani (ra) said that the special reward of Salat al-Fatih is something divine which the intellect cannot comprehend. Allah (swt) says in the Holy *Qur'an*;

ويخلق ما لا تعلمون

---

[8] *al-Futuhat al-rabbaniyya*

"And He will create what you do not know". He also said;;

*****

$$\text{مثل الذين ينفقون أموالهم في سبيل الله كمثل حبة أنبتت سبع سنابل في كل سنبلة مائة حبة والله يضاعف لمن يشاء والله واسع عليم}$$

"The example of those who spend their wealth in the way of Allah it is like a grain of corn, it grows seven ears and each ear has a hundred grains, and Allah increases for whom he wishes and Allah is All-Wise, All-Knowing." (Qur'an 2:261)

*****

Shaykh Ahmad al-Tijani (ra) was informed by the Prophet Muhammad (saws) that Salat al-Fatih is not the invention of Shaykh al-Bakri (ra). Shaykh al-Bakri was asking Allah (swt) for a very long time to show him the best way of praising Prophet Muhammad (saws) and an angel came to him with Salat al-Fatih written on a leaf of light.

*****

The Prophet (saws) was reported to have said, "Whoever recites one *Salat* upon me, Allah (swt) makes ten *Salat* upon him. And whoever recites ten *Salat* on me, Allah (swt) makes hundred *Salat* upon him. And whoever recites hundred *Salat* on me, Allah (swt) recites a thousand upon him. And whoever recites a thousand *Salat* on me, he will enter Paradise shoulder to shoulder with me." However, no one knows the value of one *Salat* of Allah (swt), not to mention ten, or a hundred, or even a thousand. To attempt to value this is to value the work of Allah (swt) and its reward as compared to that of his servant. Indeed, glory be to Allah (swt), who differs from His creatures in every respect, essence and nature of work. Here therefore lies the secret and cornerstone of making *Salat* on the Prophet (saws). One *Salat* of Allah (swt) is more than enough to turn all of Hellfire into frozen ice. What then about the best *Salat* (Salat al-Fatihi)? [9]

*****

Murideen should also observe that Salat al-Fatih does not contain a *taslim*. With regard to this, Shaykh Tijani (ra) said; "That is how Allah revealed it. Whatsoever has been revealed from the Unseen, it stands independently and it does not depend on any man made formula." [10]

*****

---

9   *Ruh al-adab*
10 *al-Futuhat al-rabbaniyya*

The divine opening

There are many forms of *salawat* that do not contain a taslim that have also been received directly from the Prophet (saws), such as Salat al-Ibrahimiyya. However, for the Murid who uses Salat al- Fatih, the rewards of it are due to him when he believes and submits to Allah.

Finally, the third pillar[11] is reciting the *tahlil* (*la ilaha illa Allah*) 100 times, which is known to be the best of remembrances, according to the hadith.

The three pillars of the *wird*, mentioned above are mentioned in *Jawahir al-Ma'ani* and other books of the *Tariqa*. They are to be recited in the morning and evening.

*****

Some Frequently Asked Questions (FAQs) about Wird:

What is a Wird?[12]

A Wird (pl. *awrad*) is the selection of names of Allah or *ayat* of Qur'an which are recited repeatedly as prayers or worship.

Allah says:

"وأذكر أسم ربك وتبتل إليه تبتيلا"

"*Remember the name of your Lord and devote to Him completely.*" (Qur'an 73:8).

Did the Prophet (saws) or his Companions (*as'hab*) have a Wird?

Yes, the Prophet (saws) had numerous awrad and recited them all.

Allah says in the Qur'an:

"وأذكر ربك في نفسك تضرعا وخفية ودون الجهر من القول بالغدو والآصال ولا تكن من الغافلين"

"*Remember your Lord {O Prophet Muhammad (asws)} within yourself, with humility and awe, without loudness in voice, in the mornings and evenings. And be not of those who are heedless.*" (Qur'an 7:205).

This is the same as the Tijani Wird, which is recited in the morning and evening.

In another ayah, Allah (swt) says:

---

11 *al-Futuhat al-rabbaniyya*
12 *al-Ajwiba*

"فاصبر على ما يقولون وسبح بحمد ربك قبل طلوع الشمس وقبل غروبها ومن آناء الليل وأطراف النهار لعلك ترضى"

"Therefore be patient with what they say, and glorify your Lord with His praise before sunrise and before sunset, glorify Him during the hours of the night as well as at the ends of the day, so that you may find satisfaction." (Qur'an 20:130).

Allah (swt) also says:

"واصبر نفسك مع الذين يدعون ربهم بالغداة والعشي يريدون وجهه ولا تعد عيناك عنهم تريد زينة الحياة الدنيا ولا تطع من أغفلنا قلبه عن ذكرنا واتبع هواه وكان أمره فرطا"

"Keep yourself content with those who call on their Lord morning and evening seeking His Face; and let not your eyes turn away from them desiring the attraction of worldly life; and obey not him whose heart we have made heedless of Our remembrance, who follows his own desires and goes to extremes in the conduct of his affairs." (Qur'an 18:28).

Shaykh Abubakr siddiq Yusuf of Ilorin, Nigeria, said that this *ayah* shows that the Prophet (saws) gave a Wird to his Companions because Allah (swt) ordered him not to take his eyes off those who call on their Lord morning and evening, seeking His face.

This action of restraining and devoting yourself totally and completely to Allah (swt), seeking knowledge of Him, is referred to as *tarbiya* in this *Tariqa*. In a hadith narrated by 'Umar bin al-Khattab, the Prophet (saws) said[13]:

قال رسول الله صلى الله عليه وسلم

"من نام عن حزبه أو عن شيء منه فقرأه ما بين صلاة الفجر وصلاة الظهر كتب له كأنما قرأه من الليل"

قال أبو عيسى الترمذي: هذا حديث حسن صحيح

"Whoever oversleeps in time allocated for his portion of *hizb* (collection of supplications a Muslim has committed himself to) in the night, and then he recited it between *subh* and *zuhr* time, Allah will write it for him as if he had recited it during the night." (Sahih Muslim).

---

13 *Ahzab wa awrad*

Shaykh Muhammad al-Hafiz comments that this hadith clearly shows that the Companions were performing specific *awrad* on a daily basis as taught to them by the Prophet (saws), and it also encourages them to make them up when missed.

*****

Rules of the Tijani Awrad:

- *The Morning Wird*: the period of the morning Wird is from Dawn to Noon, and it can still be done before sunset. Thereafter, it has to be made up (*kaffara*)..

- *The Evening Wird*: the period is from afternoon until after evening, and it can still be recited before Fajr the next day.

- In special circumstances, the Murid may recite the Wird of the following day in the night before. One should ask their *shaykh* or *muqaddam* about such exceptions.

- Always observe the Morning *Wird* before the Evening *Wird*, and observe that bringing the *Wird* forward is only accepted during the night, not the day. Our Shaykh (Ahmad al-Tijani) is reported to have said in *Jawahir* al-Ma'ani that worship at night is 500 times more rewarding;

- *Murideen* should know that making up the *awrad* that they have missed is obligatory on them. Sayyida 'a'isha (ra) is reported to have said that there is a great punishment on the one who leaves their worship because of complacency and laziness. There is also a hadith of a servant who became very ill and Allah (swt) ordered the Angels to write for him what he was used to do regularly, and was impeded from doing due to his illness.

- Women during menstruation, after giving birth and anybody who is sick to the point of being incapable, performing the *Wird* is optional for them.

- As for the Murid with a light illness (e.g. common cold, allergies), they have to recite the *Wird* in its time frame or make it up.

- And when a Murid loses or doubts their count during the *Wird*, s/he starts from the lowest denomination. The reason why the Shaykh advises the Murid to start from the lowest denomination is because when in doubt, it is best to build on certainty, which is what has already been completed (i.e. the lowest denomination). For instance, when one recited the Name of Allah "*Ya Latif*" 129 times, it is better to start with the odd 29 times, then continue with the remaining 100. The Murid recites the *Istighfar* 100 times with the intention of correction.

- When a Murid increases upon the *Wird* by mistake (adding an extra *salawat* or istighfar), s/he also recites Istighfar 100 times with the intention of correction.

Obligatory Litanies (awrad) of the Tariqa Tijaniyya

When a Murid has decreased the *Wird* by mistake, s/he has to recite what s/he has omitted and then recite *Istighfar* 100 times with the intention of correction.

- When a Murid recites the *Wird* in incorrect sequence, s/he has to start from the beginning again and thereafter recite *Istighfar* 100 times with the intention of correction.

- The Murid who loses attentiveness during his *Wird*, s/he may recite the *Jawharat al-Kamal* three times, attentively facing Qibla, after the *Wird*. Many among the 'Ulama' and Awliya' said that the only part of one's worship that will be rewarded is the part on which concentration is maintained. However, Allah (swt) has favored the Tijani Murid with the blessing of three recitations of *Jawharat al-Kamal* to make up for the reward of attentiveness s/he has lost during the Wird.

- When the Wird has been intentionally increased or decreased or said in an incorrect sequence, then it is considered invalid.

- As for the *Jawharat al-Kamal*, it can never be recited without full ablution (*wudu*), not even once. And it has to be performed in a place with enough space for seven people, including the Murid.[14]

Rules of the Wazifa:

It has four Pillars:

1. *Reciting istighfar [astaghfiru'llah al-Azim alladhi la ilaha illa Huwa al-hayy al-Qayyum]* **30 times**. Meaning: "I seek forgiveness from Allah The Immense! There is no god but He, The Living, The Self-Subsistingly Eternal.

2. *Reciting Salat al-Fatihi* **50 times**. This Salat cannot be replaced. Beginners are exempted from Wazifa until Salat al-Fatihi has been memorized, as it has been mentioned in *Jawahir* al-Ma'ani.

3. *Reciting the tahlil* **100 times**.

4. *Reciting Jawharat al-Kamal* **12 times**.

Jawharat al-Kamal:

اللَّهُمَّ صَلِّ وَسَلِّمْ عَلَى عَيْنِ الرَّحْمَةِ الرَّبَّانِيَةِ وَالْيَاقُوتَةِ الْمُتَحَقِّقَةِ الْحَائِطَةِ بِمَرْكَزِ الْفُهُومِ وَالْمَعَانِي، وَنُورِ الْأَكْوَانِ الْمُتَكَوِّنَةِ الْآدَمِي صَاحِبِ الْحَقِّ الرَّبَّانِي،

الْبَرْقِ الْأَسْطَعِ بِمُزُونِ الْأَرْبَاحِ الْمَالِئَةِ لِكُلِّ مُتَعَرِّضٍ مِنَ الْبُحُورِ وَالْأَوَانِي،

وَنُورِكَ اللَّامِعِ الَّذِي مَلَأْتَ بِهِ كَوْنَكَ الْحَائِطِ بِأَمْكِنَةِ الْمَكَانِي،

---

14 *al-Futuhat al-rabbaniyya*

The divine opening

اللَّهُمَّ صَلِّ وَسَلِّمْ عَلَى عَيْنِ الْحَقِّ الَّتِي تَتَجَلَّى مِنْهَا عُرُوشُ الْحَقَائِقِ.

عَيْنِ الْمَعَارِفِ الْأَقْوَمِ صِرَاطِكَ التَّامِّ الْأَسْقَمِ.

اللَّهُمَّ صَلِّ وَسَلِّمْ عَلَى طَلْعَةِ الْحَقِّ بِالْحَقِّ الْكَنْزِ الْأَعْظَمِ.

إِفَاضَتِكَ مِنْكَ إِلَيْكَ إِحَاطَةِ النُّورِ الْمُطَلْسَمِ.

صَلَّى اللهُ عَلَيْهِ وَعَلَى آلِهِ، صَلَاةً تُعَرِّفُنَا بِهَا إِيَّاهُ

Oh Allah! Praise with peace the Spring of the Divine Mercy, the Purest and most Immaculate Gem, the One who encompasses the center of understandings and meanings, the light of existence of all the beings, He is son of Adam, the True Possessor of Divinity, the Brightest Lightning guiding the most profitable rain clouds which fills all rivers and vessels that are openly exposed. He is Your Bright Light that fills up Your creations and encompasses all places.

Oh Allah! Praise with peace the Spring of Truth from which the Streams of Realities are manifesting, the Pure Gnostic Knowledge itself, and Your most Upright Straight Path.

Oh Allah! Praise with peace the Appearance of the Truth by the Truth, the Greatest Treasure. Your blessings comes from You to yourself; the All-Encompassing Treasured Light. May Allah praise him and his family a praise that will lead us to knowing him..

Practices that Beautify the Wird and Wazifa:

- Reciting the following verses once after the completion of Salat 'ala al-Nabi in both the *Wird* and *Wazifa* (at the end):

سبحان ربك رب العزة عما يصفون وسلام على المرسلين
والحمد لله رب العالمين

"Glorified is your Lord, The Lord of might from what they ascribe to Him, and peace be upon the messengers, and praise be to Allah The Lord of the worlds." (Qur'an 37:182)

- Reciting (سيدنا محمد رسول الله عليه سلام الله) after completing the recital of the *tahlil* whether in *Wird* or *Wazifa*.

Then complete the *Wazifa* with the *Du'a Khatm al-Wazifa* (Supplication to seal the *Wazifa*), as prescribed by Shaykh Ibrahim Niasse.

*****

Obligatory Litanies (awrad) of the Tariqa Tijaniyya

The Supplication to Seal (Close) the Wazifa:

دعاء يقرأ بعد الوظيفة للشيخ إبراهيم نياس رضي الله عنه

بسم الله الرحمن الرحيم

اللهم أنت الأول فليس قبلك شئ ، وأنت الآخر فليس بعد شئ ،

وأنت الظاهر فليس فوقك شئ وأنت الباطن فليس دونك شئ ،

فكن لنا يا أول يا آخر يا ظاهر يا باطن ولياً ونصيراً أنت ولينا ومولانا

فنعم المولى ونعم النصير ،

اللهم إنا نسألك بفاتحية الفاتح الفتح التام ، وبخاتمية الخاتم حسن الختام ،

اللهم إنا نسألك من الخير كله عاجله وآجله ماعلمنا منه ومالم نعلم ،

ونعوذ بك من الشر كله عاجله وآجله ماعلمنا منه وما لم نعلم ،

اللهم إنا نسألك الجنة وما قرب إليها من قول وعمل

ونعوذ بك من النار وما قرب إليها من قول وعمل،

اللهم إنا نسألك العفو والعافية والمعافاة الدائمة في الدين والدنيا والآخرة ،

اللهم إنا نسألك رضاك ورضى نبيك ورضى الأشياخ و رضى الوالدين ،

اللهم اجعل ما نحب فيما تحب ، اللهم اجعل فى اختيارك إختيارنا ولا تجعل إلا إليك إضطرارنا

يـاربـنـا يـاخـالـق الـعـوالـم

حـل بيننـا وبيـن كـل ظـالـم

واجز لكل مـن إلينـا أحسن

وجـازه عنـا الـجـزاء الـحسنـا

اللهم ارفع عنا الجهد والجوع والعرى واكشف عنا من البلاء ما لايكشفه غيرك .

The divine opening

ربنا آتنا فى الدنيا حسنة وفى الأخرة حسنة وقنا عذاب النار ،

ربنا لا تؤاخذنا إن نسينا أو أخطأنا ربنا ولاتحمل علينا إصراً كما حملته على الذين من قبلنا ، بنا ولاتحملنا ما لاطاقة لنا به ، واعف عنا واغفرلنا وارحمنا ، أنت مولانا فانصرنا على القوم الكافرين ،

ربنا لاتزغ قلوبنا بعد إذ هديتنا وهب لنا من لدنك رحمة إنك انت الوهاب ،

ربنا إننا سمعنا منادياً ينادي للإيمان أن آمنوا بربكم فآمنا ، ربنا فاغفر لنا ذنوبنا وكفر عنا سيئاتنا وتوفنا مع الأبرار ، ربنا وآتنا ما وعدتنا على رسلك ولا تخزنا يوم القيامة إنك لاتخلف الميعاد ،

ربنا ظلمنا أنفسنا وإن لم تغفر لنا وترحمنا لنكونن من الخاسرين ، ربنا آتنا من لدنك رحمة وهيئ لنا من أمرنا رشداً ، رب هب لنا من أزواجنا وذرياتنا قرة أعين وأجعلنا للمتقين إماماً

اللهم اغفر لحينا وميتنا وكبيرنا وصغيرنا وذكرنا وأنثانا وحرنا وعبدنا وحاضرنا وغائبنا وطائعنا وعاصينا .

اللهم صل على سيدنا محمد الفاتح لما أغلق والخاتم لما سبق ناصر الحق بالحق والهادي الى صراطك المستقيم وعلى آله حق قدره ومقداره العظيم .

سبحان ربك رب العزة عما يصفون وسلام على المرسلين والحمد لله رب العالمين

أمين

Meaning;

Oh Allah! You are The First; there is nothing before You. And You are The Last; there is nothing after You. And You are the Visible One; there is nothing above You. And You are The Invisible One; there is nothing beneath You. Oh The First, The Last, The Seen and the Unseen, be for us our aid and our supporter. You are our Chief, and what a Great Chief and Supporter You are.

Oh Allah! We ask You by the Opening of al-Fatih, grant us a complete opening. And by the closure of al-Khatim, grant us an excellent ending.

Oh Allah! We ask You from all Your goodness, from the near and the far, and from what we know and what we don't know; and we seek refuge in You from the evil in all things, the near and the far, and from what we know and what we don't know.

Oh Allah, we ask You to grant us paradise, and that which will keep us near to it, from our speech and actions. And to protect us from Hell Fire, and the speech and actions that will lead us to Hell Fire.

Oh Allah! We ask You to grant us pardon and wellbeing and perpetual clemency in the religion, the worldly affairs, and the Hereafter.

Oh Allah! We ask You to be pleased with us, Your Prophet to be pleased with us, and our Shuyukh and parents to be pleased with us.

Oh Allah! Make us to love what You love. And to make our choices Your choice. And do not make us to need anyone other than You.

Oh our Lord! Oh the Creator of the worlds!

Protect us from our oppressors.

And reward all those that have done good towards us.

And pay him on behalf of us, a great payment.

Oh Allah! Protect us from hunger and nakedness, and remove the calamities that befall us, because You are The Only One that can remove it.

Oh our Lord! Give us the best of this world and the best of the Hereafter, and protect us from the punishment of Hell Fire.

Oh our Lord! Do not hold us accountable for our forgetfulness and mistakes. Oh our Lord! Do not place a burden on us that we cannot carry, like You have placed on those before us. Oh our Lord! do not make us bear that for which we have no strength. Pardon us, forgive us, have mercy on us, You are our Chief and our supporter against the unbelievers.

Oh our Lord! Don't make our hearts to deviate after You have guided us, and grant us from Your Mercy, verily You are the Giver.

Oh our Lord! We have heard someone calling towards faith, saying; "Believe in your Lord" so we believed. Oh our Lord! Forgive us our sins, remove from us our evil deeds, and make us die with the righteous.

Oh our Lord! Give us what You have promised us through Your messengers. And do not disappoint us on the Day of Judgment. Verily You do not break Your promise.

Oh our Lord! We have wronged ourselves. And if You do not forgive us and have mercy upon us, we will be amongst the losers.

Oh our Lord! Give us from Your mercy, and dispose of our affairs in the right way.

The divine opening

Oh our Lord! Grant from our wives and our children that which will make us happy. And make us leaders for the pious.

Oh Allah! Forgive our living, and our dead, our big and small, our males and females, those present and those absent, those who are free and those in servitude, our obedient and our disobedient.

Oh Allah! Praise with peace our Master Muhammad, the One whom has opened that which was closed, and sealed that which has passed, the Supporter of the truth with the truth, and the Guide to your straightway. And bless his family. And these blessings may it be according to his true position with you and his magnanimous value.

*****

Rules of Wazifa:

1. It is recited once a day, in the morning or evening.[15]

2. Reciting it in congregation is preferable.

3. The *Wazifa* can only be performed in a state of ritual purity (*wudu'*). If one is not in a state of ritual purity or has performed a dry ablution (*tayammum*), replace the recitation of Jawharat al-Kamal with Salat al-Fatihi 20 times.

4. But if one recites it twice a day with permission, it is of great benefit. The time frame would be the same as the *Wird*.

5. If one has an excuse, the *Wazifa* can be brought forward and performed at night for the next day.

6. Whoever misses *Wazifa* will have to make it up.

7. If the sequence of the *Wazifa* is mistakenly added to, omitted from, or distorted, recite the *Istighfar* 100 times after to correct the mistake.

8. Start with the smallest denomination when there is doubt and correct it by reciting the Istighfar 100 times after *Wazifa*.

9. When reciting the *Wazifa* in congregation and mistakes occur, the muqaddam leading the *Wazifa* takes the responsibility of correcting the mistakes and there is no fault on the other attendees.

10. When an obligatory, congregational Salah takes place while the *Wazifa* or the *Wird* are taking place, pause and join the Salah, and then continue the *Wird/Wazifa* immediately after the final *Taslim*.

---

15 Shaykh Ahmad al-Shinqiti; al-Futuhat al-rabbaniyya

11. When one joins the *Wazifa* late, they should continue with them until the final (12th) recitation of the *Jawharat al-Kamal*. Before the concluding salutations (*taslimat*) are completed, the latecomer should recite what s/he was absent for, just like in Salah. For example, if one arrives during *Wazifa* and the congregation was on the sixth recitation of the Jawharat al-Kamal, the make-up of *Wazifa* would be as follows:

    - Recite with them until 12th recitation of Jawharat al-Kamal is finished (do not go on with "*Inna'Llaha wa 'l- mala'ikatuhu…*")
    - Then start from the *Istighfar* of the Wazifa 30 times
    - Then recite *Salat al-Fatihi* 50 times.
    - Afterwards, recite the *Tahlil* 100 times.
    - Then, recite the remaining Jawharat al-Kamal (in this case, six times).
    - The reciter does not need to recite the Isti'adha (i.e. *a'udhu bi-Llahi…*) nor Surah al-Fatihah.

12. One cannot perform Salah and *Wird* with one *Tayammum*.

13. One cannot recite Jawharat al-Kamal whether in *Wazifa* or outside *Wazifa* with *Tayammum*, nor in an unclean area. However, it can be replaced in Wazifa with 20 recitations of Salat al-Fatihi.

14. If, while performing the evening Wird, one remembers that the morning Wird was not performed, then he/she must stop and restart with the intention of making up the morning *Wird*. After making it up, then proceed with the evening performance of the *Wird*.

15. If, while performing a present-day's *Wird*, one remembers that the *Wird* from another day was never completed, then that *Wird* becomes necessary to make up after completing your present *Wird*, without stopping it, because the time of that one has expired.

16. A traveler can recite the *Wazifa* and *Wird* in a moving vehicle. However all movement should come to a halt when it comes time to recite the Jawharat al-Kamal, if possible. In such case where stopping the vehicle is impossible (e.g. airplane, train, boat), replace the Jawharat al-Kamal with 20 recitations of Salat al-Fatihi.

Dhikr al-Jumu'ah:

The period of *Dhikr* al-Jumu'ah is between *'Asr* and *Maghrib* every Friday. It typically starts one hour before *Maghrib* in most Tijani communities. The *Dhikr* consists of an indefinite amount of reciting the Tahlil (*la ilaha illa Allah*) before the time for Maghrib prayer comes in.

The first step starts with reciting the *isti'adha* and the *Basmala*: **(A'udhu bi-Llahi min as-shaytan ar-rajim bismi'Llah ar-Rahman ar-Rahim)**

Thereafter, recite *Surah al-Fatihah once* and *Salat al-Fatihi three times*. Then:

> *(Subhana Rabbika Rabbi al-'izzati 'amma yasifun wa salamun 'ala al-Murs-Alin wa al-hamduli'llahi Rabbi al-'alAmin)*

And then proceed with the tahlil (*la ilaha illa Allah*) non-stop until Maghrib comes in. When Maghrib comes due, end (in unison) with the salawat:

> *Sayyidina Muhammad ar-Rasulu'llah 'alayhi salamu'llah*

then:

> *(Subhana Rabbika Rabbi al-'izzati 'amma yasifun wa salamun 'ala al-Murs- Alin wa al-hamduli'llahi Rabbi al-'alAmin)*

Then the *Muqaddam* leading the *Dhikr* al-Jumu'ah will lead the closing supplication. Thereafter, **the congregation will recite Surah al-Fatihah aloud in unison, then Salat al-Fatihi three times, then conclude with;**

> *(Subhana Rabbika Rabbi al-'izzati 'amma yasifun wa salamun 'ala al-Murs- Alin wa al-hamduli'llahi Rabbi al-'alAmin)*

*****

As for the rewards of *Dhikr* al-Jumu'ah, Allah says in the Holy *Qur'an*:

"فإذا قضيت الصلاة فانتشروا في الأرض وابتغوا من فضل الله واذكروا الله كثيرا لعلكم تفلحون"

> "And when the prayer is ended, then disperse through the land and seek the bounty of Allah, and remember Allah much, so that you may prosper," (62:10).

This Ayah highlights the importance of remembering Allah on Friday evenings. There are also a hadith from the Prophet (saws) that indicates this special time when supplications are accepted.

*****

CHAPTER Four

The ethics of the Tijani Instructor (Muqaddam) and the Aspirant (Murid):

Every Tijani must know that following the ethical points mentioned in this chapter will guarantee the Murid success in this Tijani Path. No Murid will arrive at this goal without good behavior (*adab*).[16]

Adab generally means beautifying yourself with every good behavior and to abstain from every bad behavior. *Adab* has been classified into three types: (1) The *adab* of the aspirant (*Murid*) with Allah; (2) The *adab* with the shaykh and (3) the *adab* with their fellow Tijani brothers and sisters.

Adab with Allah

The first type of *adab* is to hold onto the Din, by doing what should be done and stopping where one should stop (*taqwa*), and following the *Sunna* of the Prophet (saws). By doing this, Allah will be pleased with the Murid and they will be among the first ones to enter Paradise.

Adab with the Shaykh

As for the adab with the shaykh/a, you have to respect him or her, openly and secretly, never criticize them, and always hold them in high esteem, after the Prophet (saws).

---

16 *al-Fat'h al-rabbani*

Categories of *Shuyukh*:

Know that *shuyukh* are classified into three categories:

1. *The one that takes oaths of allegiance (bay'a) from a Murid, he or she is the shaykh/a to whomever gives bay'a to them.*

And the Murid will never have spiritual benefit if they do not believe in their shaykh/a as having everything they need for their spiritual guidance, because Allah is the One Who gives to the Murid according to their intention and loyalty to the mediator, who is the shaykh/a. Thinking that your shaykh/a is incomplete will make your benefit from Allah incomplete on the basis of a lowly opinion.[17]

Shaykh al-hajj 'Abd Allah Niasse (ra) initiated Shaykh Ibrahim Niasse (ra) into Tariqa Tijaniyya, who was also his father. Although Shaykh Ibrahim (ra) reaffirmed his chain of authority (*silsilah*) with Shaykh Ahmad Sukayrij (ra), he never stops addressing Shaykh 'Abd Allah Niasse (ra) as his *shaykh*.

*****

2. *The shaykh/a that administers spiritual training (tarbiya), thereby linking the Murid with Allah, is called al-shaykh murabbi. This person must have the capability of guiding the Murid to Allah and appointing the Murid as a muqaddam. Some of these shuyukh have spiritual disclosures (kashf), and others do not have this quality.*

3. *The last category is al-Qutb al-zaman (the Pole of the Time), whom all the shuyukh are answerable to. This person may be known or unknown, but no time period will exist without him existing. He is the true Khalifa of Shaykh Ahmad al-Tijani (ra) and Prophet Muhammad (saws).*

This Qutb will only appear in Tariqa Tijaniyya, because it is the Tariqa of the time, also known as "the Tariqa of the 'Ulama'".

The Murid can have any of the above categories as their shaykh/a, and should persevere constantly with the shaykh/a while they are alive. The Murid should believe that their shaykh/a is everything and sufficient, regardless of the latter's category. This is the *adab* that guarantees the Murid to receive from Allah all that is promised by Shaykh Ahmad al-Tijani (ra). Allah is the giver and Allah is complete. The 'Ulama' of Tariqa Tijaniyya always advise the Murid to remember that the

---

17 *Qasd al-sabil*

The ethics of the Tijani Instructor (Muqaddam) and the Aspirant (Murid):

Tijani Murid worships Allah, not the shaykh. However, in order to worship Allah correctly, the intimate knowledge of knowing Allah (*ma'rifa*) has to be attained through a shaykh.

****

- When sitting in the company of one's shaykh, one should not sit boastfully (ex: legs sprawled out, slouched or in cocky posture, touching or hitting the shaykh in a "friend-like" way).

- One should not constantly sleep when in their presence.

- One should not talk too much nor without cause in their presence.

- One should not sit in the same place they sit (i.e. rug, sofa) or use their beads (tasbih)

- One should not insist on a matter after inquiring of them. It is best to believe the shaykh/a is well aware of it and leave it in Allah's Hand.

- It is strongly recommended to consult one's shaykh/a prior to plans of travel, marriage or other matters of importance.

- It is also meritorious to makes things convenient for the shaykh/a when walking (e.g. open doors ahead of them, keep pace behind or alongside them)

- One should not mention the shaykh/a in front of known enemies, with the intent to cause consternation (*fitna*)

- One should not involve oneself in the affairs nor interactions with the enemies of the shaykh/a.

- Do not let anyone slander or demean the name and character of your shaykh/a, and defend them in their absence as in presence.

- One should constantly cultivate their love for the shaykh/a, in order to gain their love and blessings.

- Be patient with the shaykh/a when they show harshness or indifference towards you.

- One should be carefully vigilant of their ego (nafs) and avoid asking self-serving questions (ex: "Why does my shaykh/a favor this person, but they did not do the same for me?")

- Do not spy on the shaykh/a in their actions, be they worship or mundane.

The divine opening

- One should not interfere in the privacy of the shaykh/a unless explicit permission is granted.

- One should try to be in a state of ritual purity (wudu') when in the presence of the shaykh/a.

- One should always be aware of their thoughts in the company of the shaykh/a, and try to keep them as positive as possible.

- One should not overburden the shaykh/a with mundane issues (ex: personal family affairs, financial needs, social engagements).

- One should avoid bringing the shaykh/a any displeasure.

- One should not marry the widow/er or divorcé/e of the shaykh/a.

- One should obey the shaykh/a in every matter s/he commands you to do.

- One should always attribute one's blessings in your life to the providence that Allah (swt) has placed in them for you.

- One should avoid thinking that, by offering the shaykh/a a gift, that one did them a favor. By thinking this, it implies that the Murid has done Allah a favor, and Allah (swt) is sufficient to Himself (al-Ghani). When the Murid gives anything to the shaykh/a solely for the pleasure of Allah, they should know that Allah is the Recipient of the gift before it reaches the shaykh/a. So know that Allah returns more than what the Murid gives.

*****

It has been reported in a hadith that Sayyida 'a'isha (ra) perfumed a coin before giving it to a beggar. When she was asked why she did that she replied, "This gift will arrive in Allah's Hand prior to the beggar's hand." It is the whispering of Shay- tan and sickness of the heart that leads the Murid to doubt or question whether his or her gift will be used correctly.

*****

- A Murid should know that the goodness of the shaykh/*muqaddam* could never be repaid in this lifetime, such as the good spiritual state one enjoys or the proximity to Allah (swt) that the shaykh has led the Murid to

- One should never think or act as if they are better than the shaykh/a, even if the Murid finds that later in life they are given a higher position than that of their shaykh/a. This high position is because Allah has accepted their prayers on behalf of the Murid.

The ethics of the Tijani Instructor (Muqaddam) and the Aspirant (Murid):

- The Shaykh has a share in all the goodness the Murid obtains.

- When undertaking *tarbiya*, a Murid is prohibited from visiting other shuyukh until it is completed (as mentioned in *al-Kharida* by Shaykh al-Dirdir). Shaykh Tafsawi in *Fat'h al-Rabbani* quotes Shaykh Sha'rani classifying a Murid into three categories, in regard to visiting other shuyukh:

1. *The Murid who visits other shuyukh, and in their heart, thinks the shaykh/a whom they are visiting is higher in rank than their own shaykh/a who has given them a Wird. This Murid has betrayed their shaykh/a.*

2. *The Murid who visits other shuyukh and has a low opinion of the shaykh/a whom they are visiting, holding only their own shaykh/a in high esteem. This Murid has wronged the shaykh/a being visited.*

The Murid who visits and has a neutral opinion over both shuyukh. This Murid has lost nothing.

*****

Shaykh Baye hayba of the first *Zawiya* of Shaykh Ibrahim Niasse (ra) in Mauritania is quoted to have said that it is best for the Murid to see all shuyukh, Muqaddamun and *Murideen* as friends of Allah. Shaykh al-Tafsawi (ra) further advises the Murid to hold a high esteem for all Muqaddamun.

When a Murid wants to link his or herself to their *muqaddam*'s shaykh/a or the Khalifa of Shaykh Ahmad al-Tijani (ra), one should do it respectfully. Shaykh Ahmad al-Tijani (ra) has said, "The *Murideen* should feel free within themselves." This means the Tijani Murid has the choice of drinking from any of the Tijani *Awliya*'.

*****

When a Murid finds themselves being stopped by their shaykh/a in regard to visiting other shuyukh, one should not think that this is a sign of jealousy or subjugation; rather, the shaykh/a is protecting them and knows what is best for them.

Adab with fellow Tijani Brothers and Sisters

- A Murid should always shake the hands of the brothers (sisters among themselves) when you meet them and after *Wazifa*.

- One should not abstain from nor boycott a Tijani brother or sister.

The divine opening

- One should love and respect all Tijaniyyin, regardless of perceived stature, rank, or chain of connection.
- A Murid should not be selfish by keeping everything for themselves, except that which Allah has especially given to them spiritually.
- One should love for their fellow Tijani what they love for themselves.
- One should visit another when they are sick.
- A Murid should inquire about or Murideen when they are absent.
- One should always think of their fellow Murideen as better than oneself.
- A Murid should humble oneself regarding other Murideen in the heart and deeds.
- One should always seek their happiness and spiritual pleasure.
- One should not compete with others for worldly achievements.
- One should help them in remembering and loving Allah.
- A Murid should overlook another's faults and forgive their wrongdoings.
- One should hide the other's secrets.
- One should love the other's close associates and hate their enemies.
- One should advise the younger ones and learn from the senior ones.
- One should not comfort oneself when the other is seen in trouble and discomfort.
- One should serve fellow *Murideen*, even by straightening their shoes.
- One should not undermine other *Murideen*.
- A Murid should not place a burden on another that they cannot maintain.
- One should not push them to a position of apology.
- A Murid should try to show balance and equity in the attention and affection they give to other *Murideen*.
- One should honor their rights at all times. Shaykh Ahmad al-Tijani (ra) said, "*Whoever is tested with breaching the rights of his brothers, surely he has breached the right of Allah.*" Shaykh Ahmad al-Tijani (ra) also said, "*The position of friendship and brotherhood are very high.*" In Surah al 'Imran (3) AL-

The ethics of the Tijani Instructor (Muqaddam) and the Aspirant (Murid):

LAH said, "*Remember the favor of Allah unto you, when you were enemies to each other, then He joined your hearts together, thus you became brothers by His favour.*"

"وأذكروا نعمة الله عليكم إذ كنتم أعداء فالف بين قلوبكم فأصبحتم بنعمته إخوانا"

Sayyidina 'Umar ibn al-Khattab (ra) said, "*You should always be with a brotherhood of truth, you will live well amongst them. During the time of safety they are decorations for you, and in adversity they are your weapons.*"

The Attributes of a *Muqaddam*/ah

- First, they should have authentic permission and proof to initiate others into the Tariqa (in writing, witnesses, or otherwise).
- They should know the rules of *Islamic* ritual purity (e.g. tahara, wudu', ghusl, tayammum), conditions and rules regarding prayer (Salah) with a good grasp of its fiqh, and all the conditions relating to the Tariqa, its pillars and its history.
- They should know the reason why Tariqa is necessary.
- They should know why somebody should have a Shaykh.
- They should know the benefits that are derived from having a Shaykh.
- They should know that all the gnosis (ma'rifa) and unveilings (kashf) of the shaykh comes from Allah (swt).
- They should teach the *Murideen* to be constantly with their shaykh for the purpose of gaining ma'rifa.
- They should be capable of disallowing somebody into the Tariqa who came for anything other than Allah (e.g. special prayers, money, fame).

*****

Note: Muqaddamun from the silsila of Shaykh Ibrahim Niasse (ra) must have completed the first levels of *tarbiya*.

*****

These attributes are the minimum requirements of what is needed for being a *muqaddam*, and whoever does not fulfill these prerequisites cannot be a muqaddam/ah. If these prerequisites are met, then the *muqaddam*/ah can give the Tariqa to somebody who accepts it with all its conditions and promises. While physically

The divine opening

giving the Tariqa to somebody, the muqaddam/ah has to picture Shaykh Ahmad al-Tijani (ra) and give on behalf of the Shaykh (ra).

- Muqaddamun should be religious people, and carry this responsibility with seriousness.

- They should never desire to be Muqaddamun. It is better for them to be chosen for this than for them to ask for it.

- They should have piety and mercy on people in general.

- They should be reliable and should be able to maintain trust (*amana*).

- They should be able to boost the morale of people.

- They should exude confidence in Allah and make people who associate with them experience this confidence.

- They should constantly be of good behavior and good conduct in all their affairs.

- They should not see themselves higher than the *Murideen* taking the Tariqa, but should be humbled by this honor.

- They should not look at the people that are taking Tariqa for the purpose of finding faults in them, rather they should be praying for them and their success.

- When they find a Murid in violation of the *Shari'a* or Haqiqa, they should not discuss this with other Tijani *Murideen*. They should try to speak about these situations without mentioning names of the *Murideen*. The wise have said, "Whoever shows you your faults between you and him, he has advised you; but whoever shows you your faults in public, he has exposed you."

- They should be a good example by reforming themselves openly and secretly. If they do not do this, they will be responsible for the shortcomings that are found in their *Murideen*.

- They should not expect any worldly benefits from the *Murideen*. If they find themselves in these conditions, they should be conscious that this is measured as a very low spiritual condition and should immediately turn to Allah (swt) in penitence (tawba) and reform themselves. The great Shaykh Hasanayn al-Tafsawi (ra) said that these Muqaddamun should not be focused on allegiances (bay'a), but instead should be focusing on rectifying their affairs.

- They should always remember that the position of being a *muqaddam*/ah is by the virtue of Prophet (saws) and Shaykh Ahmad al-Tijani (ra).

- Shaykh Ibrahim Niasse (ra) advised the Murid "*to consider himself as a light switch.*" Know that the switch of the light is unimportant when the light is shining.

- Muqaddamun should never be proud of themselves, but they may be proud to be servants of Allah, as quoted by Shaykh Mahy Cissé (may Allah preserve him).

- Muqaddamun should always remember and exemplify the Spiritual Station of 'Abd Allah (saws) in their actions (always strive to be the best servant of Allah, a advocate of good manners, constantly having a clean heart). They should remember they are the servants of the Servants of Allah.

- Muqaddamun should be an example for their *Murideen*, inwardly and outwardly.

- Muqaddamun should always keep contact with the *Khulafa'* of the Tariqa, and its Special People.

- Muqaddamun should not fight each other, speak ill of each other, or compete with each other in worldly affairs.

- The Muqaddamun should condemn and avail against jealousy with other Murideen and Muqaddamun. Constantly fighting this vice will give them victory over it, by the blessing of the Prophet (saws) and the blessings of Shaykh Ahmad al-Tijani (ra). If a *muqaddam* finds difficulties in abstaining from jealousy and bad thoughts regarding others, they should immediately repent and be satisfied with the decision of Allah. They should always remember that Allah's decision in their affairs is better for them.

We advise all Muqaddamun and *Murideen* to constantly read *Spirit of Good Morals (Ruh al-adab) by Shaykh Ibrahim Niasse (ra)*, and inculcate these morals one at a time into their behavior, inwardly and outwardly, until they have perfected it. Only then will they achieve high positions in the presence of Allah.

Types of Muqaddamun:

Muqaddam: This *muqaddam* can initiate a person into Tariqa Tijaniyya; however, they cannot promote someone else to become a *muqaddam*.

Muqaddam 'Ashra: This *muqaddam* can promote no more than ten Tijani Murideen to become a *muqaddam*.

Muqaddam Mutlaq: This *muqaddam* may initiate people into the Tariqa, as well as promote them to *muqaddam* without limitations.

The divine opening

Are women allowed to give initiation into the Tariqa?

Women can be Muqaddamun once they fulfill the above conditions. *Islam* has regarded women as a full and equal partner of men in bearing personal and common responsibilities, and in receiving rewards for their deeds. *Islam* has given women a leading role in many instances. Never in the history of *Islam* has any Muslim doubted the human status of women nor their fine spiritual qualities.

Allah says in the Holy *Qur'an*[18]:

"وإذ قالت الملائكة يا مريم إن الله اصطفاك وطهرك واصطفاك على نساء العالمين"

"Oh Maryam! Surely Allah has chosen you, purified you and preferred you over the women of the worlds." (Qur'an 3:42)

Allah also says:

"والذاكرين الله كثيرا والذاكرات أعد الله لهم مغفرة وأجرا عظيما"

"...and the men who remember Allah much and the women who remember, Allah has prepared for them forgiveness and a great reward." (Qur'an 33:35)

Allah says:

"ومن يعمل من الصالحات من ذكر أو أنثى وهو مؤمن فأولئك يدخلون الجنة ولا يظلمون نقيرا"

"And whoever does righteous deeds, whether a male or female – provided he or she is a believer – shall enter paradise and will not be wronged a speck." (Qur'an 4:124)

عن أم ورقة رضي الله عنها ان النبي صلى الله عليه و آله و سلم

أمرها ان تؤم اهل دارها

رواه ابوداود و صححه ابن خزيمة

And in a hadith, the Prophet (saws) permitted Umm Waraqa (ra) to lead prayer in her house (Sunan Abi Dawud).

---

18 *al-Ajwiba*

The ethics of the Tijani Instructor (Muqaddam) and the Aspirant (Murid):

The Tariqa Tijaniyya permits women to be Muqaddamun by virtue of the aforementioned *ayat* and *hadith*.

*****

LETTERS OF SHAYKH IBRAHIM NIASSE (RA) TO HIS MUQQADAMUN

The first letter:[19]

In the Name of Allah, the Most Gracious, The Most Merciful:

All praise and thanks belongs to Allah, The Lord of all the Worlds, The Most Gracious, The Most Merciful. May the peace and blessings of Allah be upon our master Muhammad (saws), according to his true reality —and his magnitude is extremely great!

As'salamu 'alaykum wa rahmatu'Llahi ta'ala wa barakatuhu! I have received your letter which you sent and I am very happy about its content. I am entrusting your care to Allah, whose safekeeping is eternal, and I am advising you to attach your heart to Allah in all of your movements and moments of rest. Be for Allah ! "Whosoever is for Allah , Allah is for him!" Cast aside the entirety of creation in your service to the Real — and your own ego [nafs] is also from among the created beings! **"Say: 'Allah!' Then leave them to play in their vain discussions and disputes." (Qur'an 6:9)**

You should know that (in this Qur'anic verse) Allah has described everything other than Him as "sport and play" [khawdan wa la'ban]. You should therefore take for yourselves two (2) shuyukh: your "shaykh" in the zahir should be the Book of Allah and the Sunna of His Messenger (saws) and your Shaykh in the batin is our master Ahmad al-Tijani, may Allah be well-pleased with him — and he is always with you! However, the means are only the means, no more! What I just said was meant for you (the person the letter is addressed to). I am advising you to conceal your secret and bury what Allah has entrusted to you from the 'Mysteries of His Lordship' [sirru rabubiyya], until Allah causes you to appear. Whosoever lays claims to being a "shaykh" before the appearance of permission from Allah has destroyed and lost his Din and his worldly matters, and he will be exposed and degraded among his community! However, if Allah causes you to appear, there is no one who can prevent His Gift!

The love of appearance [hubb al-zuhur] before its proper time will cut you off from appearing at all because of the share you have allowed the ego [haz al-nafs]. If Allah has kept you hidden, then being hidden is what is best for you; and if He makes you

---
19 *Jawahir al-rasa'il Shaykh Ibrahim*

The divine opening

to appear, then appearance is what is best for you! Do not want or desire except that which Allah wants and desires! Whosoever desires to be known then he is really the servant of appearance, and whosoever desires to remain hidden is really the servant of concealment. But whosoever only desires what is the desire of Allah is the real servant of Allah! The gnostic ['arif] is the one who has abandoned his will for the will of Allah!

Say to Hadi that I have given him permission to teach you the 'Secret of Visitation' [Sirr al-Ziyara] — and it is one-third of the Mysteries, and it includes the Name which is specific to the spiritual station of Shaykh Ahmad al-Tijani, may Allah be well-pleased with him. My greeting of peace should be given to the Khalifa habibullah Seck. I am requesting that he pray for us. Salam.

Ibrahim ibn al-Hajj 'Abd-Allah (Niasse) al-Tijani

1929 CE | 1348H

The second letter:

In the Name of Allah, The Most Gracious, The Most Merciful: May the peace and blessings of Allah be upon our master Muhammad (saws) and also upon his Family and Companions.

All praise and thanks is due to Allah, Who has made following His Awliya' (a condition) of success and righteousness! He who has made loving them, venerating them and obeying their commands (a condition) for what is profitable and beneficial!

Peace and blessings be upon the Master (saws) of this life and the next, the one who said: "Islam has been built upon five pillars: to bear witness there is no god except Allah and Muhammad is His Messenger; to establish the five daily prayers [Salat]; to fast (the month of Ramadan); to pay the alms-due [zakat]; and to perform the pilgrimage to Makkah if one is financially able."

May Allah be pleased with his absolute inheritor [Shaykh Ahmad al-Tijani], who said: "If you hear anything attributed to me, weigh it in the scale of the Sacred Law [Shari'a]; if it conforms to the Shari'a, then accept it; and if it does not, then reject it!"

After this: I am advising myself and all of you with what Allah has advised the previous communities — to have conscious awareness of Allah [taqwa] in public and in private! The (basic meaning of) taqwa is to obey the commands and avoid the prohibitions of Allah. The most important of His commands is the observance of the five daily prayers in congregation and on time — along with the purification by water. The most amazing thing is for a person to claim a relationship to Allah and to our Shaykh Ahmad al-Tijani, may Allah be well pleased with him, and then

The ethics of the Tijani Instructor (Muqaddam) and the Aspirant (Murid):

to be neglectful about His prayer or to be heedless about its (pre-requisite) purification— such as performing purification by means of clean soil [tayammum] for prayer, falsely claiming an excuse. The (valid) excuse for tayammum does not last (past one obligatory prayer) and it cannot become generalized behavior for an entire community! Verily, we are from Allah and to Him is our return! "**So repent to your Creator and kill yourselves [nafs], that is better for you with your Creator,**" (Qur'an 2:54).

After this: I am writing this letter to all of my beloved ones in the city of Jamain, the place of our righteous father Ahmad Kurk and Abubakar Bittéy and his brother Muhammad, and our lover Fajik Cham, and Muhammad Bittéy and Muhammad Mijakeen, and everyone else including their names and their surnames, the common and the elite, and everyone else in general.

As'salamu 'alaykum wa rahmatu'llahi ta'ala wa barakatuhu! A greeting which is carried by the support of our master Ahmad al- Tijani, may Allah be well-pleased with him. I am asking Allah to refine and rectify our spiritual states and our destinies, and to grant us the sweetness of faith, and to bestow upon us the sincerity of our worshipful service [sidq al-'ubudiyya], along with maintaining the rights of Lordship [huquq al-Rabubiyya]. I am asking Him to inscribe our names in the Register of His Beloved and Chosen Ones [diwan ahbab wa asfiya'] and to protect and watch over us, surely He is the Guardian of the righteous!

I am advising all of you to congregate with the brethren for the recitation of the daily Wazifa, for whosoever among you abandons it for even one time without a valid Law-based excuse after receiving our letter should know that I am free of him, and he has nothing to do with us and we have nothing to do with him! Verily, no one can rightfully be said to travel in our Tariqa except by acting as myself and my companions are doing. You must constantly renew your repentance all of the time — at every spiritual station — along with diligent observance of Allah (muraqaba), with the passage of every breath and every moment! You must act on the saying of the Prophet (asws), "Hold yourselves to account before you are brought to account!" You must strive with all sincerity in your dealings with your Lord and Master, so that none of you are found where He has prohibited, nor negligent with what He has commanded.

I am warning all of you to avoid approaching any of the forbidden things, as the haram things are the neighbors of the Hellfire! I am also warning you about heedlessness [ghafla], because heedlessness is the origin of every sin, lust, and ugly behavior.

The Real has said, "Good behavior [adab] is expected of whosoever I have unveiled My Names to, and total annihilation is due from the person I have unveiled the perfection of My Essence to!" Therefore, I dvise all of you to have good adab in your spiritual wayfaring [suluk]! As the poet said: "A spiritually- enraptured mystic [majdhub] has become rebellious if he has failed to sober up, and if he does not correct

The divine opening

himself with obedience he has abandoned guidance. He who obtains what is desired must rush to gratitude; if not, then the severance of his spirit (from the Divine Presence) is only the beginning of his ruin!"

Therefore, I am advising all of you to occupy yourselves (totally) with Allah by rejecting everything other than Allah! I am advising all of you to hold to patience; to love one another; to guide one another; to visit one another; to show humility to one another; and to sit with one another—in Allah, for Allah, and by Allah! Assist one another in righteousness [birr] and taqwa, and remember Allah with much remembrance, in order that you may be successful! Save your family and yourselves from the Hellfire, and the Prophet (saws) said, "That is to say to your family: 'Guard your prayer!', 'Guard your prayer!' 'Guard your fasting!', 'Guard your fasting!' 'O family, Purify yourselves! 'O family, provide for the poor!'" Allah says, **"Order your family to establish the prayer, and to be patient in its performance. We do not ask from you provision, rather it is We Who provide for you and the good end belongs to those who are consciously aware of Allah," (20:132).**

You should know that all of you must praise and thank Allah because He has made you to be among the first people to enter this Divine Effulgence [Fayda]; but do not sit and relax or become comfortable, because there are people coming after you who will outstrip you if you become negligent in performing the rights of your Lord! Seek refuge in Allah from that occurring because it will be the greatest loss! The goal of this (Faydah Tijaniyya) is the constant spiritual elevation and increase with the passing of every moment! I advise you to keep your Zawiya active with the establishment of the five daily prayers and the recital of the daily Wazifa. I advise you to spend all of your (free) time in sending prayers and salutations upon the Messenger of Allah (saws) with Salat al-Fatihi (lima ughliq), for whosoever does this has obtained the greatest success! Salam.

Transcribed by Sidi 'Ali ibn al-hasan Cissé from the dictation of Shaykh Ibrahim Niasse (al-Tijani)

1930 CE | 1349H

The third letter:

I am sending a greeting of peace, which is free of vanity, nonsense and sin, to my noble son, the lofty Sharif "Shaykhani" Manna Abba wuld al-tulba. I have received your letter that conveys your state of well-being, and this is the most valuable news I have received!

All praise and thanks belongs to Allah! We are also in good health and well-being, and we are enjoying constant increase — both outwardly and inwardly! All praise and thanks belongs to Allah!

The ethics of the Tijani Instructor (Muqaddam) and the Aspirant (Murid):

As for what you mentioned concerning the growth and increase of disciples [Murideen], we thank and praise Allah, who has caused the increase of Iman in the Ummah!

As for the question of spiritual training [tarbiya] — may Allah guide us and you — know that tarbiya in our Tariqa is by the spiritual zeal [himma] of Shaykh al-Khatm Ahmad al-Tijani, may Allah be well-pleased with him, the one who said: "Whosoever would know me, must know me by myself alone!" So there is nothing for an authorized muqaddam to do except explain the conditions (of the Tariqa) and its correct comportment [adab].

Likewise, there is nothing for a disciple [Murid] to do except to preserve and maintain the known religious obligations and perform the obligatory remembrances, the Wird al-lazim, Wazifa, and dhikr al-Jumu'a, holding full conviction that the Wird al-lazim is the greatest secret of Tariqa Tijaniyya!

A disciple must hasten to its performance and diligently continue to perform whatever extra litanies and remembrances that they are able to obtain permission for after the Wird al-lazim, desiring nothing except the Noble Countenance of Allah — not anything in this life or the next world, nor any of the varying spiritual stations [maqamat] — but only witnessing the Bounty and Grace of Allah!

A Murid must persist in having a good opinion (of Allah and His servants) and completely submit all of one's affairs to Him. If you are able to persevere in this without any other goal, you must eternally praise and thank Allah for it! The worst condition for a disciple to have, and the most depraved state of worshipful service [qadih fi al-'ubudi-yya] and the greatest shame and disgrace of the self, is when a person worships and remembers Allah with a sense of entitlement and expectation of spiritual illumination [Fat'h]; today or tomorrow or in one week or in one month or in one year! No one should think to deserve or merit anything from Allah, but should think that He is deserving to be worshipped for His Essence alone! Whosoever feels entitled to experience spiritual illumination or feels it to be slow in coming should repent to Allah! You must know that if you spent your entire life in the worship and remembrance of Him and then experienced the Illumination for a single moment, you would realize in that single moment what is equal to your entire life or even greater! Even if the Spiritual Illumination never occurs you should be content that your life was spent in the remembrance of Allah, for there is nothing due from a disciple except to thank and praise Allah in every state! I am asking Allah on behalf of myself, you and all of the brethren that He grant us safety, good health and contentment with the decree of Divine Providence. Salam.

(Shaykh) Ibrahim ibn al-Hajj 'Abd-Allah al Tijani

Kaolack, Sénégal; 1935 CE | 1354H

P.S.

As for my spiritual support ['umdati] in the Tariqa Tijaniyya, you should consult my book entitled **Kashif al-ilbas** and understand (it) well!

*****

COUNSEL OF SHAYKH AHMAD AL-TIJANI (RA) FOR THE MUQADDAMUN

I advise every muqaddam to forgive his brothers mistakes and pardon their faults and shortcomings, avoid hostility with them and to mediate and settle their disputes. Remove the causes of enmity between them, and destroy the fire of fitna amongst them. Do all of this just for the pleasure of Allah, not for any worldly gain. He should prevent his Murideen from gossip; and if he sees one of them gossiping, he should try to put an end to it with wisdom. He should treat them with soft and easy companionship. He should avoid being harsh and difficult with them in any instruction towards Allah and their brothers. The Prophet (saws) has said:

يسروا و لا تعسروا و بشروا و لا تنفروا

"Be soft, don't be harsh and encourage them, and don't push them away."

The muqaddam should keep away from their worldly earnings, and should not turn his attention to their belongings. All his belief should be that Allah is the Giver and the Withholder, and He raises and lowers whom He desires. The muqaddam should also advise his Murideen not to be superfluous with their wealth. He should never demand anything from them, not even a little, except what they offer without injury to them, because the thoughts of mankind are always surrounding the worldly affairs.[20]

---

20 al-Fat'h al-rabbani

CHAPTER
Five

The Criticisms regarding the Tariqa Tijaniyya:

Criticisms[21] have proven to be ineffective in causing decrease to the status and influence of the Tariqa, and have, ironically, increased its prestige. If a critic has truly pure intentions, void of any vile qualities, he would know that all servants of Allah have faults and should look unto himself first. Shaykh 'Abd al-Wahhab al-Sha'rani, a great Shafi'i scholar from Egypt, said, "Human beings are made from imperfections and faults, these things were brought together and are called human being." We should always remember this when looking at other servants faults. Shaykh Ahmad al-Tijani (ra) said, *"Lies will be created in my name. If you hear anything attributed to me, weigh it in the scale of the Sacred Law [Shari'a]; if it conforms to the Shari'a, then accept it; and if it does not, then reject it!"*

There are three categories of critics: The first category comprises of the one who sticks to his ideology without reasoning; he has pride, envy and stubbornness, and he derives his criticism out of these qualities. This is the type of person we do not have anything to say to, because if we recite every Revelation (e.g Zabur, Tawrah, Injil, Qur'an) to him, he will still not reason with us.

كل العداوة قد يرجى إزالتها * إلا عداوة من عاداك من حسد

"All enmities, there is a hope for it to be gone, except the enmity originated from envy."

The second category comprises of he who criticizes with the intention of defending Islam. However, he has not fulfilled the conditions regarding criticism (i.e. he must educate himself to the extent of knowing the different opinions held amongst 'Ulama'). He must have adequate knowledge of the sciences of Islam, especially the miracles of Prophets and Awliya', and other conditions that are mentioned in

---

21 *al-Fat'h al-rabbani*

The divine opening

a book called *Shari'ah al-Jaysh*. These categories of people are rewarded for their criticisms. It is important to differentiate between who is fulfilling the conditions of the *sufi* orders and those that are using it for their own personal benefit.

The third category comprises of he who fulfills the conditions of criticism mentioned above, he has an opened mind, he is objective and his aim for criticizing is to know the truth and follow it. It is this person, who has attracted all of our attention.

The First criticism:

Is it possible to see the Prophet (saws) in broad daylight, whilst being in a complete state of wakefulness, after his (saws) demise? Shaykh Ahmad al-Tijani (ra) said that he saw the Holy Prophet (saws) face-to-face, in broad daylight, while awake and received from him the *Wird*.

The response to this criticism is YES. Clear proof is present in the Sunna, from renowned *Islamic* jurists and gnostic saints that seeing the Prophet (saws) is possible after his death.

Abu Hurayra (ra) has narrated that the Prophet (saws) said: *"Whoever sees me in a dream, verily he will see me awake, and Satan cannot take my form,"* (Bukhari, Muslim, Abi Dawud).

من رآني في المنام فسيراني في اليقظة و لا يتمثل الشيطان بي

al-tabarani also narrated a similar hadith from Malik bin 'Abd-Allah and a hadith from Abu Bakrata. al-Darani also related the same hadith from Abu Qatada. Imam Muhammad Abu Jamrah (the 'Alim who summarized sahih al-Bukhari), he commented on this hadith, he says: *"The hadith proves that whoever sees the Prophet (saws) in a dream, he is going to see him awake."* He further remarks that this hadith context *"includes dreaming about the Prophet (saws) in his lifetime and outside his lifetime, and whoever restricts the meaning of it after Prophet Muhammad (saws) has left its meaning wide open, he only troubles himself."*

al-Hafiz ibn hajar al-Asqalani said, after quoting the above hadith, that 'Ulama' have two different views in the interpretation of the matter of seeing the Prophet (saws) whilst awake. He said that al-Qurtubi's view is that seeing the Prophet (saws) awake is against logic, but Abu Jamrah views this experience by Muslims as a possibility. However, Ibn hajar completed the two ideas by saying that he sees no contradiction, because Abu Jamrah "clearly shows that this experience is only achieved by the complete *'Awliya'* and therefore this is classified under Islamic jurisprudence as a karama (supernatural event), which is acceptable by all 'Ulama'.

As for the sayings of *Islamic* jurists, ibn al-hajjaj says in his book *al-Madkhal*, that seeing the Prophet (saws) while awake is very scarce and it happens only for a few people. People of this caliber are very few these days, or maybe even none whatsoever. However, we cannot refute that this happens to some great people whom Allah protects in the seen and unseen.

Imam al-Bayhaqi, in his book *al-I'tiqad*, relates that the spirits of all the Prophets, after their death, are returned to them; therefore, they are alive with their Lord like the martyrs. The Prophet Muhammad (saws) saw many of the other Prophets when he experienced the Mi'raj (Ascension).

أخبر صلى الله عليه و آله و سلم أن

صلاتنا معروضة عليه و أن سلامنا يبلغه

و ان الله حرم على الأرض ان تأكل أجساد الأنبياء

The Prophet (saws) informed us in a hadith that whoever sends salutations upon the Prophet (saws), these salutations will be presented to him and our greetings reach him.

Allah has prohibited the earth from eating the flesh of the Prophets.

Imam al-Bayhaqi relates that al-Barizi said that: "I heard from some *Awliya'* of our time and before our time that they have seen the Prophet Muhammad (saws) while awake and alive, after his death.

As for the sayings of the saintly Poles (Aqtab), Sayyid 'Abd al- Qadir al-Jilani (ra) said: "I saw the Prophet (saws) before zuhr prayer and he said to me, 'Oh my son! Why don't you talk?' Then I said to him, 'Oh my father! I am not an Arab, how can I speak with the eloquent people of Baghdad?' Then the Prophet (saws) told me to open my mouth and he spat in it seven times, and he commanded me to speak to the people and *'call to your Lord with wisdom and good speeches,'* (Qur'an 16:125)."

(ادع إلى سبيل ربك بالحكمة والموعظة الحسنة)

Then, I prayed zuhr and I sat down and many people came to me, I tried to speak, but I couldn't speak to them, then suddenly I saw *Sayyidina* 'Ali (ra) standing in front of the gathering, and he said to me: Oh my son! Why don't you talk?" To read the rest of the story, it is found in the book titled *Bughyat al-mustafid*, by Sayyid Muhammad ibn al-'Arabi bin al-Sa'ih.

In another book titled al-Minah al-Ilahiyyah by ibn Faris, he said that he heard Shaykh 'Ali al-Khawwas saying: "When I was five years old, I read Qur'an with Shaykh Ya'qub (every day). One day while enroute to meet the shaykh, I saw the Prophet (saws) awake, not in a dream. When I saw him (saws), he was wearing white cotton. Thereafter, I suddenly found (his white garb) on myself, then he (saws) said to me, 'Read Surah al-duha and Surah al-Inshirah,' then he disappeared. When I reached 21 years, I again saw him (saws) in front of me, during my Fajr prayer, and he hugged me and said to me:

$$\text{(وأما بنعمة ربك فحدث)}$$

'And as for the favors of your Lord, proclaim it'. And from that moment I inherited the Prophet's (saws) tongue." Shaykh 'Ali al-Khawwas said that: *"No servant is complete in the station of gnosis (maqam al-'irfan) unless he meets the Prophet (saws) awake and talks to him face-to-face."*

Other shuyukh who have seen the Prophet (asws) awake are, Shaykh Abu Madyan al-Maghribi, Shaykh 'Abd al-Majid al-Qinawi, Shaykh Musa al-Rawawi, Shaykh Abu al-hasan al- Shadhili (owner of hizb al-Bahr), Shaykh Abu al–'Abbas al-Mursi (the one that said that he does not count himself a Muslim if the Prophet [saws] is out of his sight for a moment), Shaykh Abu Sa'ud bin Abu al-Asha'ir, Shaykh Ibrahim al-Matbulu, and Imam al-Hafiz Jalal al-Din al-Suyuti (Shaykh al-Hadith, who reportedly met the Prophet Muhammad [saws] awake more than seventy times). It has been said by some 'Ulama' that whoever believes it is possible, Allah blesses him with this possibility, and whoever restricts this belief, loses this blessing.

Shaykh Muhammad bin Saghir al-Shinqiti (the author of *al-Jaysh*) said Imam al-Laqqani said that: All the scholars of hadith have come to a consensus regarding the possibility of seeing the Prophet (saws) after his lifetime awake and in dream, and there is no dispute regarding it.

The Second criticism:

Regarding to the attendance of the Prophet (saws) and his four Khulafa' (ra) during the recitation of Jawharat al-Kamal. The answer to this is what we have just mentioned about the Prophet (saws) being alive after his death, and he appears wherever and whenever he wants to. Imam al-Hafiz al-Suyuti saw the Prophet (saws) in Cairo and kissed his hands. Shaykh al-Mannawi said that the Prophet (saws) attends every congregation (*majlis*) that sends *salawat* upon him. He further said that the *As'hab* (ra) and the *Awliya'* can also attend any *majlis* they wish to. Shaykh 'Ali al-Khawwas also said: "The *Awliya'* are free in their state after death."

The question arises for some seekers of tasawwuf: how is it possible for the Prophet (saws) to attend in numerous congregations, wherever and whenever he wants to? This miracle has clearly been shown to us in the hadith where the Prophet (saws) returns every greeting showered upon him at the same time. Could you imagine the amounts of *salawat* that Muslims throughout the world are sending at the same time, every second? Then imagine the Prophet (saws) returning each greeting, every second. Here lies our belief of this miracle.

In the same manner, the Angel Isra'il, the Angel of Death, takes a hundred thousand lives at the same time, in different places throughout the world, and this does not stop him from performing his worship, (*'ibada*). Therefore, it is obvious that the Prophet (saws) is in a greater position, as the most beloved Prophet of Allah, than the Angel Isra'il.

As for the Third criticism:

Regarding the spreading of the white sheet during the *Wazifa*; it is good to purify, perfume and venerate the place of dhikr, for it shows respect to the Angels (*mala'ika*), good Jinn and the special ones. Thus, the spreading of the white sheet does not have any other purpose than to show respect to Allah and those who remember Him, seen or unseen.

We therefore earnestly advise all readers not to discard the belief in the words of the *Awliya'*, even if it cannot be comprehended. Remember the experience of *Sayyidina* Musa (as) with Sayyidina Khidr (as) where he could not understand/refused to accept *Sayyidina* Khidr's actions, which were outright contradicting the Shari'a.

The Fourth criticism:

Is that the Tijani *Murideen* uphold the Jawharat al-Kamal with more veneration and honor than *Qur'an* and Salah. This is false and impossible, because Jawharat al-Kamal can be replaced with 20 recitations of Salat al-Fa- tihi, but Salah can never be replaced. A Muslim without wudu' has to perform Salah with tayammum, and the same rules apply for the recitation of *Qur'an*. The reason for the Murid reciting Jawharat al-Kamal with wudu' only not tayammum is because the special secret in it can only be achieved this way.

The Fifth criticism:

Is regards to the meaning of the word 'al-asqam' in the Jawharat al-Kamal. The critics believe that this word is derived from the Arabic word 'saqim' which means sick, and they claim that it's superlative form is 'asqam' meaning most sick, which leads to a negative connotation of praising the Prophet (saws). This view is incorrect from two angles; firstly from a grammatical point, the word 'asqam' means 'the most straight', and it is derived from the root 'qa-ma' which means 'to be straight'. This is the meaning meant in Jawharat al-Kamal. The correct superlative for 'saqim' is actually 'ashaddu saqaman'. These critics who derived this meaning are extremely far away from the real meaning of the Jawharat al-Kamal. Secondly, if this word did indeed imply sickness, then its negative connotation can never degrade the Prophet (saws). By way of explanation, consider the following narration. The Prophet (saws) is reported in a hadith to have been very sick, and a Sahaba, 'Abd-Allah, came to the Prophet (saws) and touched him

The divine opening

with his hands and he remarked: "Oh Prophet of Allah! You are very sick." And the Prophet replied: "Yes, my sickness is the like of two people's." In this hadith we conclude that the Prophet's (saws) sickness is twice heavier than a normal person. So what is it for the Best of Creation (saws) to be sick, in comparison to a regular person?

The Sixth criticism:

Has to do with, why wudu' is required for a *Wird* which is not obligatory in Islam? In a hadith reported by Abu Dawud, we find the Prophet (saws) made tayammum just to answer 'Wa 'alaykum as-salam' to somebody that greeted him, and then he apologized by saying I did not want to mention Allah's name while not with ablution. This is why whenever we speak to Allah during Salah , *dhikr*, reciting Qur'an or salawat, we will have wudu' or tayammum. Once a righteous man saw the Prophet (saws) in his dream and asked if the salawat is always accepted? The Prophet (saws) answered that salawat will never be rejected when the person holds a state of purity (wudu' or tayammum). Through this we know that whoever talks to Allah with wudu' or tayammun has good *adab*.

The Seventh criticism:

Has to do with the bounty (fadl) of Shaykh Ahmad al-Tijani (ra) (e.g. his feet being on the necks of all the *Awliya*', he is the seal of the *Awliya*', he supplies all the Aqtab and *Awliya*' spiritually through the Prophet (saws), and that all Awliya' and Aqtab drink from his ocean). The answer to all these statements is that the Prophet (saws) informed Shaykh Ahmad al- Tijani (ra) that he is the Hidden Pole (al-*Qutb* al-Maktum) and the Seal of the Saints (al-Khatm al-*Awliya*'). The one who supplies the Gnostic knowledge (ma'rifa) to all Awliya' from Adam to the day the trumpet is blown. Thus as you can see, the Wali with this special position is definitely above the necks of all *Awliya*'.

Shaykh Ahmad al-Zarruq said that Shaykh 'Abd al-Qadir al-Jilani deserved the Qutbaniyya of his time because he achieved three qualities that no one of his time achieved, at one and the same time, i.e., he was the most knowledgeable of his time, his level of worship was like no one else of his time, and he was a grandson of the Prophet (saws) (as referenced from the book *al-Tutiyya fi bayan fadl as-Shaykh 'Abd al-Qadir al-Jilani*). When looking at Shaykh Ahmad al-Tijani (ra), we find an extra quality (i.e. him being the seal of the *Awliya'*), as he was informed by the Prophet (saws).

The Eighth criticism:

Is regarding Shaykh Ahmad al-Tijani's followers being better than the As'hab of Prophet (saws). The answer is that this assertion is impossible because Shaykh Ahmad al-Tijani (ra) said when he was asked: "Is a Wali with kashf better than a

The Criticisms regarding the Tariqa Tijaniyya:

Sahaba without kashf?" Shaykh al-Tijani (ra) answered: "A Sahaba with no kashf is better than a Wali with kashf." Shaykh al-Tijani (ra) continues by narrating the hadith of Prophet (saws) that "if one person should give in charity all of mount 'Uhud in gold, he will never reach my As'hab, not even close."

The Ninth criticism:

Has to do with, why Shaykh al-Tijani (ra) makes such powerful statements about himself in public? Some people are of the opinion that he should have kept these gifts in secret. Firstly, our response is that Shaykh Ahmad al-Tijani (ra) made the *Murideen* aware of his position as shown to us by Prophet Muhammad (saws) in his lifetime. The Prophet (saws) has said about himself: *"I am the Prophet without boast, and I am the son of 'Abd al-Muttalib".*

أنا النبي لا كذب أنا اب عبد المطلب

Narrated by Bukhari

In another statement, he said: *"I am the master of all human beings, (and I say this) without boast."*
In another statement, he (saws) said: *"I am the first person to be raised in the Day of Rising, and the first to enter Paradise."*

أنا سيد ولد آدم ولا فخر ، وأنا أول من تنشق عنه الأرض و انا اول من يدخل الجنة

Narrated by Muslim.

And in another statement, he said: *"I am the most knowledgeable of Allah amongst you, and also the one who fears Allah the most."*

أنا أعلمكم بالله و أتقاكم له

Narrated by Bukhari

In addition, in the Qur'an, Prophet Yusuf (as) asked Allah, *"Set me over the treasures of the earth, verily I will protect it, and I am knowledgeable."*

قال اجعلني على خزائن الأرض إني حفيظ عليم

(Surah Yusuf, Verse 55)

The author of *al-Kashf* said after explaining the ayah:

(قال لا يأتيكما طعام ترزقانه إلا نبأتكما بتأويله قبل أن يأتيكما)

"Before any food comes, I will surely reveal to you the truth."

The divine opening

The two prisoners were informed by the Prophet Yusuf (as) of what food they would receive that day, before it even arrived. This is how they started to believe in him. The author said that if a scholar explains himself and discloses of his gifts, this does not mean that he is boasting as Allah has prohibited us in the *Qur'an*:

$$ (ولا تزكوا أنفسكم) $$

Meaning: **"Don't praise yourselves."** Illustrated above, Prophet Yusuf (as) exposed himself and his gift out of necessity.

The second reason why Shaykh Ahmad al-Tijani (ra) proclaimed the bounties of Allah was in order to thank Allah, in collaboration of the ayah in Qur'an, Surah al-duha:

$$ (وأما بنعمة ربك فحدث) $$

"Proclaim the bounties of your Lord!"

The Tenth criticism:

Is regarding recital of the *Wazifa* and *Dhikr* al-Jumu'a audibly. Our critics draw attention to the hadith where the Prophet (saws) said:

$$ (خير الذكر الخفي) $$

"The best of dhikr is the silent one".

Imam al-Hafiz al-Suyuti in his book, *Natijat al-fikr*, addresses this issue with many *ahadith* showing the significance of reciting *dhikr* audibly. One of these aHadith is when the Prophet (saws) said:

$$ (أكثروا ذكر الله حتى يقولوا مجنون) $$

"Make a lot of dhikr, until people call you crazy".

Imam al-Suyuti comments that if you think about this hadith, you will understand that nothing is wrong with making *dhikr* aloud. It further proves that making *dhikr* aloud is desired by Allah. The hadith advising us that the best *dhikr* is the silent one, Imam al-Hafiz al-Suyuti compares this hadith to the hadith of reciting *Qur'an* silently:

$$ فقد ثبت في الصحيح عنه صلى الله عليه وسلم أنه قال: $$
$$ لا يؤمن أحدكم حتى أكون أحب إليه من والده وولده والناس أجمعين. $$

The Criticisms regarding the Tariqa Tijaniyya:

"The reciting of Qur'an silently is like giving charity secretly".

Again, in this hadith, it does not stop the reciter from reciting aloud. This proves that Allah does not prohibit making audible *dhikr*. Imam al-Nawawi proposed two stipulations, wherein silence is preferred when one fears showing off, which leads to pride or one may disturb people who are praying or sleeping nearby. When these circumstances are not present, reciting audibly is preferred. The reason for this is that the listeners benefit from the dhikr, in that it joins the hearts, gathers the reciters' thoughts, calls their attention to Allah, and adds strength to their fight against sleep. Imam al-Ghazali (ra) shared the same idea as Imam al-Nawawi in his book *Ihya' 'ulum al-Din*. Imam ibn 'Ata'illah al-Iskandari said in his book *Miftah al-falah* that if the reciters are in congregation, the best way to recite their dhikr is aloud with the same rhythm and in unison. It is recorded that Ibn 'Abbas (ra) said that the raising of voice with dhikr after the obligatory prayer happened in the time of the Prophet (saws).

روى البخاري و مسلم عن أبي معبد مولى ابن عباس أن ابن عباس رضي الله عنهما أخبره أن رفع الصوت بالذكر حين ينصرف الناس من المكتوبة كان على عهد النبي صلى الله عليه وسلم، وقال ابن عباس : كنت أعلم إذا انصرفوا بذلك إذا سمعته

Narrated by Bukhari

The Prophet (saws) has said that Allah (swt) has said: *"Whoever mentioned Me within himself, I mention him within Myself; and whoever mention Me in a gathering, I mention him in a greater gathering."*

روى مسلم عن أبي هريرة رضي الله عنه قال: قال رسول الله صلى الله عليه وسلم: قال الله تعالى: أنا عند ظن عبدي بي، إن ذكرني في نفسه ذكرته في نفسي، وإن ذكرني في ملأ ذكرته في ملأ هم خير منهم

Narrated by Muslim

It is also mentioned in another hadith that when Abu Bakr al-siddiq (ra) was reciting his prayer softly, and *Sayyidina* 'Umar (ra) was reciting loudly. The Prophet (saws), after listening to them both, asked, *"Abu Bakr, why are you reading softly?"* He answered, *"Allah, the One who is listening, can hear me."* Then the Prophet (saws) turned to ask Sayyidina 'Umar (ra) why he was reading aloud, and he replied, *"I am waking the sleepy, and driving away the shayatin, and I am pleasing Allah."* The Prophet (saws) then ordered Abu Bakr al-siddiq (ra) to raise his voice and ordered 'Umar (ra) to lower voice. We can see Sayyidina Abu Bakr (ra) was asked to recite louder, and Sayyidina 'Umar was asked to recite softer to unify their intentions and actions.

The divine opening

Therefore, the critics should learn not to dispute with the *Awliya'*, because that would mean they are fighting Allah. In sahih al-Bukhari, Abu Hurayra (ra) relates that the Prophet (saws) said, "*Allah has told me: 'Whoever fights my Wali, I have declared war on him.'*"

(من عادى لي وليا فقد آذنته بالحرب)

If you find in their words or their deeds anything contradictory to the *Shari'a*, then come up with seventy excuses for it. You know that these people who are *'Arifin*, they fear Allah the most amongst His creation, so their words and actions may have hidden reasons and meanings that only Allah (swt) and the Wali know, as in the story of Prophet Musa and Khidr (as) in Surah al-Kahf.

*****

The Eleventh criticism:

Is, why do Tijanis specify numbers for our dhikr in the *Wazifa* and *Wird*? The critics argued that Shaykh Ahmad al-Tijani (ra) invented these numbers, and that the Prophet (saws) didn't fix any number for *dhikr*, which is understood to be supererogatory (nafil), ergo against the Sunna.

The answer to this is the hadith of the Prophet (saws) where he says:

أحب الأعمال الى الله أدومها و إن قل

"*The most beloved worship to Allah is the constant one, even if it is small.*" (sahih al-Bukhari and Muslim)

Shaykh Muhammad al-Hafiz al-Misri explained, "If you do not specify a number for yourself the quantity of the worship cannot be constant."

In another hadith, the Prophet (saws) says that:

"اكلفوا أنفسكم ما تطيقون فإن الله لا يمل حتى تملوا"

"*You should commit yourselves to the quantities you are able to execute, and Allah will not get tired (from your worship), but you will.*"

*****

CHAPTER
Six

Bounties for the Sincere followers of Tariqa Tijaniyya:

1. Whoever dies with this Tariqa will die upon *Iman* and *Islam*.[22]
2. Allah (swt) will ease their death for them.
3. They will only see light in their graves.
4. They will be under the shade of the Throne ('arsh) of Allah (swt).
5. They will cross the Ethereal Bridge (sirat) faster than a wink of an eye and on the shoulders of the Angels.
6. Allah (swt) will quench their thirst from the Vase of the Prophet (asws).
7. They will live in the Heights of Paradise ('Illiyin) in the neighborhood of the Prophet (saws).
8. Whoever loves al-Shaykh (Ahmad al-Tijani) will not die except as a Wali.
9. The parents, wives, parents-in-law and the children of a Tijani Murid will be forgiven, provided that they did not curse, or hold enmity against the Shaykh.
10. Anything that hurts the Murideen hurts the Prophet (saws).
11. Whenever they perform the dhikr, 70,000 angels will accompany them and participate in their dhikr and all the reward of this will be written for them.

*****

---

22 *Futuhat al-rabbaniyya*

The divine opening

These bounties and blessings are directed towards good, consistent Muslims practicing the Tariqa Tijaniyya, who die on this path of constant Prayer and Purification. We advise the Murid to consider these bounties as an encouragement to take the *Wird* Tijaniyya seriously, but not as a guarantee from Allahs punishment, for indeed, our Tijani Saints feared Allah the most. No one knows in what state they will die. Many enter *Islam* and the Tariqah and leave both as well, wa nauzu billah. Shaykh Hassan Cisse (ra) has always advised us to never feel safe, and often quoted the statement of *Sayyidina* 'Umar (ra) that "Even if I find myself with one foot inside Paradise, I will never feel safe." Prophet Adam (as) was inside Paradise and Allah (swt) put him out!

CHAPTER Seven

The position of Shaykh Ahmad Tijani

فضل الشيخ رضي الله عنه

The Prophet (saws) said to Shaykh Ahmad al-Tijani, *"You are the Hidden Pole (al-Qutb al-Maktum),"* and that was said to him while he was awake, not in a dream. The *Murideen* then asked him, "What does the word 'hidden' mean?" He replied by saying, *"The one whom Allah (swt) hides from all His creation, including the Angels and Prophets, except the Master of Existence (i.e. the Prophet Muhammad [saws]). He is the one who completely has all of what the Awliya' have (and aspire to)."* Shaykh Ahmad al-Tijani also said, *"I am the Master of all Awliya', just like the Prophet (saws) is the Master of Prophets. Every saint ,from the start of Creation until the day the Trumpet will be blown, drinks from Our ocean."*[23]

Shaykh al-Tijani also said, pointing with his index and middle fingers, *"He and I are like this (referring to the Prophet [saws] and himself). The Prophet's (saws) soul nourishes all the Prophets and Messengers (may peace be upon them all), and mine supplies all the Aqtab, 'Arifin and Awliya' from the beginning and forever."*

The statement of the great Shaykh 'Abd al-Qadir al-Jilani (ra) was related to Shaykh Ahmad al-Tijani (ra), wherein Shaykh al-Jilani (ra) said that his feet are on the shoulders of every saint. When Shaykh al-Tijani (ra) heard this, he was reclining, and then sat up straight and said, **"Shaykh al-Jilani's feet were on top of the shoulders of every saint of his time. As for me, my feet are on top of the necks of every saint from the time of Adam (as) until the Trumpet is blown."**

Shaykh Ahmad al-Tijani (ra) also said that whatever blessings flow from the Essence of the Prophet (saws) to the other Prophets come to me in like fashion, and then to all Creation. Shaykh al- Tijani (ra) also said that the Prophet (saws) taught

---

23 *al-Futuhat al-rabbaniyya*

him a special Knowledge that is shared between the two of them, and no one knows this Knowledge except Allah. Shaykh Ahmad al-Tijani (ra) received this special knowledge during his lifetime and in a waking state.

Shaykh Ahmad al-Tijani (ra) further relates that there is a difference between the positions of al-*Qutb* al-Maktum and the Mahdi, and clarified that he is not the Mahdi. "The person with this position has yet to arrive, and he is going to be a just leader from this Ummah, but not a saintly axis (*Qutb*)."

CHAPTER
Eight

Frequently Asked Questions (Faqs)

Answered by:

Imam Fakhruddin Owaisi al-Madani
('Alim and Tijani *Muqaddam*)
Cape Town, South Africa

Q: What acts nullify the *Wird* and *Wazifa* while reciting them?
A: **Acts such as breaking wudu', talking unnecessarily, or reciting something else.**

....

Q: What should one do if wudu' is lost during the *Wird* and/or *Wazifa*?
A: **If it is lost during the Wird, one should go make wudu' again and start over from the beginning.**

If it is lost during the Wazifa and one is reciting it alone, he/she has to make wudu' again and start over from the beginning.

If it is lost during the Wazifa and it is being recited in a congregation, then he/she must go make wudu'. Upon returning to the congregation, he/she continues the dhikr with everyone else. When the 12th and final recitation of the Jawharat al-Kamal is completed, he/she MUST make up every other

recitation (i.e. Istighfar, Salat al-Fatihi, Tahlil) that was missed while he/she was away renewing their wudu'.

Q: Is it obligatory [wajib] to face the Qibla while reciting the *Wird* and *Wazifa*?
A: **No, it is only highly recommended [mandub].**

Q: If someone is called upon (e.g. parents, spouse, phone calls) during the performance of the *Wird* or *Wazifa*, how should one respond?
A: **It is only permissible to respond to ones Shaykh, parents and husband (not wife), especially if the latter are unaware of the adab of dhikr. As for anyone else, one cannot answer them except with a non-verbal gesture to indicate that you are busy reciting the dhikr.**

Q: Is it permissible to resume the *Wird* and/or *Wazifa* if one had to interrupt it for some reason?
A: **If it was a short and valid interruption, such as a few words to a parent or joining congregational prayer [Salah fi jama'], then you may continue from where you stopped. If it was a long or unacceptable interruption, then you must start over again.**

Q: What should one do if he/she lost count or mistakenly recited more than what was necessary (i.e. reciting the Salat al-Fatihi 103 times)?
A: **One should continue from the minimum number that he/she is sure they recited. After being done with the Wird or the Wazifa, he/she should recite the Istighfar 100 times as atonement.**

Q: Are mistakes like forgetting to say "Muhammadun Rasulu'llah 'alayhi salamu'llah" after completing the *Wird* forgiven?
A: **Yes, but do not become careless or frequent with them. Small mistakes become big when done continuously.**

Q: Can I perform the *Wird* and/or *Wazifa* sitting on a chair or sofa?
A: **It is better to sit on the floor, per the Sunna of the Habib (saws), and as an act of humility.**

Frequently Asked Questions (Faqs)

It is allowed to recite the Wird or the Wazifa sitting on a chair up to the 6th recitation of the Jawharatu al-Kamal during the Wazifa to the end, here, it becomes mandatory to sit on the floor in honor of the Messenger of Allah (saws). Of course, the elderly and persons who are sick or with disabilities can recite the entire Wazifa sitting on a chair. Allah and His Prophet (saws) have excused them.

Know that there are some differences between the 'Ulama of the Tariqa regarding some of these minor issues. I have only mentioned the more prevalent view, per my knowledge and research. I also take the practice of Mawlana Sahib al-Fayda Ibrahim Niasse (ra) as the final word, for he had said:

"And this poor Slave is the Door of Shaykhuna Ahmad al-Tijani (ra). Whoever I accept, Shaykh Ahmad al-Tijani (ra) accepts, and whoever I reject, Shaykh Ahmad al-Tijani (ra) rejects."

....

Q: Who is authorized to lead the Wazifa?

A: Technically, any upright and sane Muslim man who is in this Tariqa can lead the Wazifa. However, in any gathering, it is the muqaddam that is requested to lead. If there are more than one qualified muqaddam, then seniority, erudition and piety are take into consideration (in that order) for the one asked to lead.

Another consideration is that if there is already an established muqaddam over the group or the assembly hall (Zawiya), then he should lead unless he asks another to lead.

Exceptions to this are when:

- The established *muqaddam* has already delegated a brother to lead.

- There is a *muqaddam* in the gathering who is also a Sharif [descendant of the Prophet (saws)]. Many shuyukh will ask him to lead even, if they are senior to him in age and more learned than him. There have been cases wherein the Sharif was very humble and insisted that the senior *muqaddam* lead; that is the way of the Noble Descendants of the Prophet (saws), as we have seen in many places.

- It is also preferable to request that *muqaddam* or whomever is leading the *Wazifa* to use the local cadence (i.e. rhythm, recitation style), out of respect and consideration of the congregation. Reciting the *Wazifa* in another cadence is unacceptable and can cause much confusion and disharmony.

- If there are no brothers in the gathering who can perform the *Wazifa* in its entirety with correct pronunciation and etiquette, then there is no need for it to be done in congregation.

Q: Is it permissible to be appointed a *muqaddam* upon taking the Tariqa?

A: One's appointment as a muqaddam is an extremely serious matter.

Many people who have the license (ijaza) to do that are abusing it. They are appointing any tom, dick and harry as muqaddam without much testing and discretion. The Tijani Master, Sidi al-'Arabi ibn al-Sa'ih (ra) , mentioned that one should not appoint anyone as a muqaddam in their entire lifetime than appoint an ineligible person!

One should not fear for the spread of the Tariqa because of this warning, for its spread is guaranteed by the blessed Prophet (saws). In any case, an ineligible muqaddam can only harm it even through his/her propagation efforts.

The Basic Conditions for a person to be made a muqaddam are:

- Be steadfast on the *Shari'a* (e.g. Salah five times a day, proper hijab and *adab*, halal means of employment and income).

- Be consistent in the Tariqa (e.g. making the *Wird* on time, *Wazifa* in congregation or daily if alone,

- *Dhikr* al-*Jumah* in congregation on Fridays, not mixing principles and practices with other turuq).

- One should have proper knowledge of the Tariqa, its history, rules and conditions, etiquettes and the mandatory litanies. There are too many people who have been appointed as or call themselves "*muqaddamun*" who did not know the correct *Adab* if you join the *Wazifa* late or missed a *wird* there are many that cannot even recite the Jawharat al-Kamal correctly.

- Be conscious of Allah (taqwa), and loving Him and trying hard to attain His pleasure and knowledge of Him.

- He/she should be in love with our Master Shaykh Ahmad al-Tijani (ra) and striving to learn as much as we can about him. He/she should not look towards any non-Tijani saint or shaykh for spiritual guidance and/or elevation.

- He/she should be willing to sacrifice their time and resources for the Tariqah, which every Murid should presently be engaged in.

- He/she should have holistic good manners (*akhlaq*) in interacting with people and the rest of creation, otherwise all of the qualities mentioned above are useless. A rude, insensitive, racist and/or destructive person should NEVER be appointed as a *muqaddam*.

- He/she should show patience (sabr) and mercy (rahma) with their Murideen, like any teacher.

Even before any of these qualifications can be considered, the one to appoint a muqaddam must be inspired by Allah (swt) to do so.

Remember that the most valuable thing we have after accepting Islam is this Special Tariqa of the Prophet (saws).

Are you ready to give it away to someone who does not deserve it?

Be reminded that there is great punishment for appointing an ineligible person as muqaddam, for these ineligible people do great harm to the Tariqa and to Islam as a whole.

However, some big shuyukh of our Tariqa do appoint some special people as muqaddam, knowing from their insight and unveiling (kashf) that this individual will soon fulfill all the conditions of being a muqaddam.

Of course, if a person ultimately does not fulfill the conditions, then their office as muqaddam is just a meaningless and empty title; and he/she should seek repentance (tawba) for their inadequacy. May Allah (swt) protect us all. Amin.

Q: Does the shaykh or *muqaddam* that supervises one's spiritual training [*tarbiya*] affect the outcome and effectiveness of it? If so, to what extent?

Yes, indeed they do! I know of people who began their tarbiya from some muqaddam, and struggled very hard to attain knowledge of Allah (swt), and often did not succeed. But when they renewed the tarbiya with Shaykh Hassan Cissé (ra), they attained the grand opening (Fat'h al-kabir) very soon thereafter!

For those in the Tariqa via the spiritual chain (silsilah) of sahib al-Fayda Shaykh Ibrahim Niasse (ra), then the Fat'h is guaranteed after the completion of tarbiya, as a special boon from Shaykh Ahmad al-Tijani (ra).

It all depends on the spiritual level and sincerity (ikhlas) of the muqaddam who oversees one's tarbiya. But sometimes, the problem is not the muqaddam, but one's own insincerity and laziness.

We have to ask ourselves: Am I really searching for Allah with all my heart? Am I ready to sacrifice everything for Him: my money, my time, my pride? Am I even capable of bearing the responsibilities of this Tariqa?

In all matters, one must have sabr. The Fat'h comes when you don't expect it, as mentioned by our Master Shaykh Ahmad al-Tijani (ra) in the treatise

Jawahir al-Ma'ani. It is hujum... it "attacks your heart unexpectedly". The tarbiya is a means of preparation and protection for it; otherwise, you will die.

Although the basic adhkar of this Tariqa are enough, one does extra to prepare ourselves and show desire for Allah. We have a lot of time in the day and especially the night. We should use as much time as we can in the Remembrance of Allah. That is the Way of the people of gnosis and intimacy with Allah (swt).

There are many Muslims that say that the five daily prayers are the limit and that extra dhikr is unnecessary and even an innovation [bida']. Some brothers and sisters in the Tariqa are complacent, as well, and say that the mandatory Wird and Wazifa are enough or too much.

However, the Practice of the Prophet (saws) and his Blessed Companions (ra), Shaykh Ahmad al-Tijani (ra) and his Noble Companions (ra), and Shaykh Ibrahim Niasse (ra) belies such people. In most of his letters, our Master Shaykh al-Tijani (ra) advised his aspirants to recite extra Salat al-Fatih on a daily basis, even giving them specific amounts and timings for it.

Q: When performing the *Wazifa* alone, does it have to be recited in the rhythm of Medina-Baye (Sénégal) or can one do it according to one's own pace?

A: One may recite the Wazifa in any style and at one's own pace, when reciting alone.

Q: If one performs the *Wazifa* every day after sunset, then for some reason cannot do it after Maghrib one day, how much time does one have to do it in order to remain in the proper time (i.e. does one have until before Maghrib on the next day to do it without it being a "make up")?

A: **If you usually do the Wazifa after Maghrib, then its performance will be valid until the Maghrib [period] of the next day. This is because the Wazifa must be done once every 24 hours. After Maghrib of the next day, you will have to do it as "make up".**

However, it is better to start the 24-hour cycle for the performance of the Wazifa from the late afternoon ['Asr]. In this case, you may delay "today's Wazifa" until after Maghrib, but may do "tomorrow's Wazifa" after 'Asr, if need be. This is more convenient and many of our shuyukh time their Wazifa in this manner.

Q: Can the morning *Wird* be done before dawn prayer [Subh], if one doesn't have time to do it after Subh?

A: The morning Wird can be done before Subh. In fact, Shaykh Ahmad al-Tijani (ra) encouraged the performance of the morning Wird, during tahajjud time, and mentioned that its reward is multiplied 500 times during the night!

The morning Wird may be recited earlier, anytime from midnight until Subh. However, if the call to prayer [*adhan*] for Subh is called while you are busy with the Wird, then you will have to re-start the Wird after prayer.

Also, if you have delayed your afternoon Wird until after midnight, then you cannot do the morning Wird in the midnight. Then it must only be done after Subh.

Q: Does the Tariqa Tijaniyya abrogate all previous turuq?

A: As narrated by Sidi al-Tayyib al-Sufyani (ra) as #101 in his work, al-*Ifadat* al-*Ahmadiyya*, Sayyidina Shaykh Ahmad al-Tijani (ra) had indeed stated that:

طريقتنا تنسخ جميع الطرق

"My Tariqa abrogates all turuq"

The 'Ulama' of the Tariqa have interpreted this statement in various ways. It should be noted that none of them interpreted it to mean that all turuq besides the Tijaniyya are invalid, as some ignorant friends and foes like to say.

Out of many, I can recall three interpretations:

1. Shaykh Ahmad bin al-'Iyyashi Sukayrij al-Fasi (ra) of Morocco interpreted this statement to refer to the well known condition of our Tariqa, that whoever wishes take the Tariqa Tijaniyya must absolutely forsake whatever s/he has from other turuq, as the Tijani Path abrogates all of that for the aspirant (reference: *al-Nafhat al-'anbariyya fi al-ajwiba al- sukayrajiyya*).

2. Shaykh Muhammad al-Hafiz al-Misri (ra) of Egypt interpreted this statement to mean that the Tariqa Tijaniyya possesses the methods, virtues and techniques of all the other turuq combined; therefore, it is the complete Tariqa in which the seeker will find all that s/he needs. Indeed, s/he can continue his spiritual journey in this Tariqa from wherever he stopped in his/her previous one (reference: al-Risalat al-jama'at al-wihda al-*Islamiyya*).

The divine opening

3. Sahib al-Fayda Mawlana Shaykh Ibrahim Niasse al-Kawlaki (ra) of Senagal interpreted it to mean that in these Last Days, no Tariqa other than the Tijaniyya will be able to provide the spiritual training [tarbiya] to gain the complete ma'rifa to the aspirants of Allah (reference: Kashif al-ilbas 'an Fayda al-khatm Abi al-'Abbas).

You should also know that this is what we have been inspired to know and believe about our Tariqa, but we have not been told to convince the whole world about it. Our Shaykh Ahmad al-Tijani (ra) clearly instructed us to respect all the turuq of the Awliya' and believe in their truthfulness and merit [*baraka*]. He (ra) also taught us that whoever disrespects any living or passed-on Wali will be thrown out of the Tijani realm. So we must be very careful! Every Tariqa is guiding people to some level of Islam, Iman or Ihsan, as the Prophet (saws) wants them to.

For more information on this matter, you can reference the following works:

- *al-Fat'h al-nurani fi bayan wajh al-insilakh 'an awrad al- mashayikh li akhdh al-wird al-Tijani by Shaykh Abu Bakr Atiq (ra) of Kano (Nigeria)*

- *Raf' al-haraj 'an man inslakaha 'an ayyi Tariqatin wa fi al-Tijaniyya indaraj by Mallam Tijani 'Uthman of Kano (Nigeria)*

....

Q: I am interested in the Tariqa, and my father is also a follower of the Tariqa. But I think that I am not ready to commit myself to the adhkar. I don't think I will have time [to do them all]. What do you advise?

A: The Tariqa Tijaniyya is a very easy Path to Allah. Its adhkar are very easy to make and do not take much time. However, they have a great spiritual effect on a human being. Every true Muslim needs them.

The Tijani dhikr, consisting of three aspects (previously detailed in this handbook) should be done after the Subh and 'Asr prayers. It is very easy and takes no more than 15 minutes.

Then there is the blessed Wazifa performed once daily, which is a bit longer and takes about 25 minutes of dhikr.

I say: If Allah is blessing us every minute and every second, then why can't we dedicate some time for Him every day? If we really love Him, then we will find the time to praise Him. For example, if you love a girl, you will always make lots of time for her?

Many others here, myself included, took the Tariqa when we were university students, and, by Allah (swt), it was the best decision we've made.

Frequently Asked Questions (Faqs)

Today, we cannot live without our daily Remembrance, and we hope Allah is happy with us.

Q: How could I get spiritual support (madad) from a shaykh? Is there a special method for it? And, what's the meaning of the prayer: *"wa amiddana bi madadi Khatmi al-Awliya' al-Kitmani?*

A: You receive madad from Rasulu'llah (saws) and our Shaykh al-Tijani (ra) by loving them, following them and reading their Wird and Wazifa. If you do that, they will love you. If they love you, they will send you the madad. Then you will see great blessings in your Din and dunya. No special prayers are required. Just be sincere in your worship and love.

The meaning of the Prayer is: *"(O Allah) Support us with the hidden support of the Seal of the Saints (Shaykh Ahmad al-Tijani)."*

You see, Allah can support us through countless ways, even through an ant or a disbeliever. However, the best of Divine support is the one that comes though the Seal of the Prophets (saws) and the Seal of the Saints (ra). That is why we ask for it like this.

The shuyukh of the Tariqa have narrated from Sayyidina Shaykh (ra) a method to 'consult' with him, by closing the eyes and turning the heart to him, and imagining one's self standing in front of him (ra). Then recite Salat al-Fatihi 100 times and mention your need to him. His (ra) advice to you will be the first thought that enters you heart.

Of course, it goes without saying that that such a 'consultation' will only work with those people who are sincere and are constantly purifying their hearts and fulfilling their duties like the Salah and awrad. Even the best cell phone will not work if there is no reception signal. Thus, the connection with Sayyidina Shaykh (ra) must be true and real.

Q: In our Tariqa, some people renew (*tajdid*) their commitment with every renowned muqaddam or shaykh they meet. Is this recommended?

A: Renewal in the Tariqa with an authorized muqaddam must be done if one breaks the rules of the Tariqa, or the muqaddam who gave them the Tariqa in the first place breaks the rules thereof. However, it may also be done for other reasons such as:

- To receive the blessing of a great descendant of the Prophet (saws) (*Sharif*), or a shaykh or muqaddam whose chain (sanad) is closer in degrees to the Prophet (saws) and Shaykh Ahmad al-Tijani (ra), particularly if they are higher in perceived (spiritual) status than your present Muqaddam/Shaykh.

- When one's primary muqaddam cannot guide them further in tarbiya and tarqiya. Thus, a person may find a shaykh murabbi and renew with him. Sidi al-Sharif Ahmad Mahmud al-'Alawi (ra), lovingly called al-Shaykhan Manna Abba, came to Sahib al-Fayda Shaykh Ibrahim Niasse (ra) in Kaolack and requested tajdid. At the time, he was al- ready a Tijani muqaddam who was ready to inherit the Mauritanian khilafa of the Tariqa from his father, al-Khalifa Sidi Muhammad al-Tulba (ra), whos spiritual inheritance came through his forefathers; al-Khalifa al-Shaykh Ahmaddu (ra) and the great Shaykh Muhammad al-Hafiz al-Shinqiti (ra), the direct and absolute Khalifa of Shaykh Ahmad al-Tijani in West Africa. So Shaykh Ibrahim (ra) refused to renew for him, saying, "I cannot give you (in this Tariqa) more than what you have already inherited from your noble forefathers." So the Sharif (ra) insisted, "I am not requesting that. I am requesting from you what Allah (swt) has granted you specifically and did not grant them (i.e. the Fayda)." Satisfied with this answer, Shaykh Ibrahim (ra) renewed the Tariqa for him and immediately gave him the litanies for spiritual training (awrad al-tarbiya). Soon thereafter, he (ra) achieved a very high status in ma'rifa and went on to become the Khalifa of the Fayda Tijaniyya in Mauritania.

Once renewal is done with a greater shaykh, it does not mean that one should cut all ties with their previous muqaddam. They must still respect him as their original muqaddam and as a Tijani brother/sister.

However, a Murid should not "play" with two Muqaddamun at the same time, unless the two are working together under a single shaykh within the same chain. If a murid comes under a complete shaykh of tarbiya in this Tariqa (i.e. Shaykh Hassan Cissé [ra]), he should obey him fully and not turn towards any other muqaddam or shaykh in the Tariqa whatsoever. Running after every muqaddam, shaykh, or miracle we hear about is very bad etiquette and kills the spiritual journey.

One should decide which muqaddam or shaykh they can trust for their spiritual development, and then stay with them. They must love and respect all in our Tariqa but stick to their murabbi, unless Allah (swt) guides them to that which is better for them.

We now live in a time when innumerable fake, unqualified, arrogant people are being heralded as great Muqaddamun, shuyukh, poles of the Age (aqtab al-zaman), and even advisors of the awaited Mahdi (wizarat al-Mahdi)! Then when the credentials of such people are questioned, it is said of them, "They are of the Malamatiyya, whose hidden spiritual

Frequently Asked Questions (Faqs)

excellence is cloaked by the outward appearance of a sinner." What is forgotten is the golden rule of Tasawwuf that a Malamati cannot be followed or given allegiance to!

A person I know traveled to one country to meet one such "shaykh al-akbar" and "al-Qutb al-zaman". When he arrived in that country, he discovered that this man had no Zawiya, no Wazifa [to preside over], no followers and no reputation in his own country amongst the other shuyukh in the Tariqa. In fact, the entire Tijani community of his country spoke bad of him and considered him to be no more than a salesman of secret prayers and rare old books, many of which were forged. He realized that not all that glitters, especially on the internet, is really gold. He regretted turning away from his real Shaykh and running after fake ones looking for miracles.

Follow your heart, and fully submit to a Complete Shaykh in Shari'a, Tariqa and Haqiqa. Anything less is a waste of time. The essential rule of Tasawwuf, and especially our Tariqa Tijaniyya, is to be focused. These rules are stated by both Shaykh al-Islam (Ibrahim Niasse) (ra) in his book <u>Ruh al- adab</u> and Shaykh Lahsan al-Baqili (ra) in his book <u>al-Ira'a</u>.

May Allah keep us steadfast and focused. Amin.

Q: What is the Tijani position on music?

A: This is a fiqh issue, and the people of the Tariqa may follow the verdicts of the various 'Ulama regarding it. The Tariqa itself does not prescribe any particular view.

According to Imam al-Ghazali (ra), there is no strong proof that prohibits the usage of any musical instruments, therefore they are all allowed per se. Based on what we saw from the Tijani saints, they preferred this opinion to that of other great 'Ulama who considered certain or all instruments as impermissible [haram]. However, all 'Ulama agree that any music that promotes haram notions (e.g. vulgarity, indecency, racism, adulterous inclinations, abuse, violence), is haram to listen to, with or without instruments.

What remains is music that promotes halal matters (e.g. love for country, history, culture, beauty of life, human emotions). This would be permissible, as long as it does not distract from our principal modes of worship [*'ibadat*] nor compromise ones Tawhid, nor is excessive. Indeed, the

The divine opening

Prophet (saws) himself listened to such things on some occasions (such as the authentic hadith of the wedding songs).

Then there is the spiritual concert [sama'] of the *sufiyya* that promotes spirituality and the higher love for the Divine Realm. This would be recommended in certain cases, when it takes our souls from the lower worlds to the higher realms. However, it should not be excessive.

Like numerous other Awliya' our Master, al-Shaykh Ahmad al-Tijani (ra), would sometimes ask his personal cantor [*munshid*], Sidi al-Jabiri (ra), to sing some sufi poems to him using the oud, as mentioned by Sidi Ahmad Sukayrij (ra) in his work <u>Kashf al-hijab</u>.

He (ra) would particularly prefer to hear the poems of the Egyptian 'arif, Ibn al-Farid (ra), who wrote:

عن مذهبي في الحب مالي مذهب

وإن ملت عنه يوما فارقت ملتي

وإن خطرت لي في سواك إرادة

سهوا على خاطري قضيت بردتي

> As for my set method in love | I have no set method
> For me, if I neglect His Love for a day, I have denounced my Religion
>
> Indeed, if I think of other than You for a moment (even by mistake) | then I consider myself an apostate

And who wrote on the Tongue of the Essential Reality of Muhammad (asws) (al-Haqiqa al-Muhammadiyya):

اني وإن كنت ابن أدم صورة

لي فيه معنى شاهد بأبوتي

> "And even if I am the son of Adam by my appearance |
> The meaning (purpose) he carries points that I am actually his father!"

Allah! Allah! Allah! May we always drink from His Divinely- Filled Ocean (saws)!

Q: One thing I've heard persistently about the Tariqa Tijaniyya is that if someone takes the Tariqa and then leaves it to join another, then all future spiritual development is cut off. How do the Tijaniyyin explain when this is not what happens? I've been informed by someone who I would consider reliable in such matters that Shaykh 'Abd al-Rahman al-Shaghuri, perhaps most famous as the murshid of Shaykh Nuh Ha Mim Keller, was a murid in the Tariqa Tijaniyya before leaving it for the Shadhiliyya after meeting Shaykh Ahmad al-'Alawi, not only becoming a murshid in the Tariqa but the successor of his own shaykh and, in essence, the highest authority for the Shadhiliyya of Syria?

A: **Know that people take a Tariqa either for merit (baraka) and attribution (intisab), or for spiritual training (tarbiya) and embarking on the road to nearness to Allah (swt).**

Technically, the Tariqa Tijaniyya is not given for only for baraka. It can only be given for tarbiya. However, there are many people who may simply take it for the baraka. Sometimes, it is difficult for the muqaddam to determine the seeker's intentions.

It seems that the respected Shaykh al-Shaghuri (ra) took the Tariqa Tijaniyya, in the beginning of his spiritual quest, for baraka only. The proof being that at the same period of his life, he took many other turuq, as well. It is obvious that he never really practiced the Tijani Way, or comprehended its realities. He probably just wanted to get ijaza in Salat al-Fatihi or be connected in some way to Shaykhuna al-Tijani (ra).

In fact, the person he took the Tariqa was a Syrian merchant named Sidi 'Ata' al-Ghabra, who was not a scholar nor person of high rapport in the Tariqa.

Such adherents are not condemned if they leave the Tariqa Tijani- yya respectfully, because they never really practiced in it in the first place. They only sought the baraka. They were eternally not meant for al-Shaykh Ahmad al-Tijani (ra). Their "training" was meant for someone else, and would hence naturally grow in another Tariqa. As long as they don't disrespect the Tijani Way, there is no blame nor detriment on them. Of course, by leaving the Tijani Way and choosing another way, they will still be spiritually deprived of the unique Openings guaranteed only for members of this Tariqa Tijaniyya.

Even if such a person became a great saintly pole [Qutb] in another Tariqa, he or she is spiritually behind the Tijani Murid. As related in Kitab al-Rimah by Shaykh 'Umar Tal al-Futi (ra), al-Shaykh Ahmad al-Tijani (ra) clearly stated - as informed by the Prophet (saws) - that, "If the greatest poles of this Umma came to know what Allah (swt) has prepared for the followers of this Tariqa, they would cry and say: 'O Allah! You gave us nothing!'" This is something that may be understood only in fleeting Divine experience [dhawq] in this world and witnessed openly in the Hereafter.

As for the person who leaves the Tariqa Tijaniyya, its awrad, or its Shaykh (ra) out of disrespect and enmity, then al- Shaykh Ahmad al-Tijani (ra) has warned that: "He will face destruction," and that, "He will die on disbelief."

May Allah (swt) protect us from such. Amin.

This is because this person has turned his back to Sayyidina Rasulu'llah (saws) himself, as the Shaykh of this Tariqa is no one but Rasulu'Llah (saws) himself, in blood and in spirit, and we recite his litany and give allegiance [bay'a] to him (saws) only.

Along with al-Shaykh Ahmad al-Tijani (ra), we are all followers of the Prophet (saws) himself. Indeed, the Prophet (saws) had told him, "Your companions are MY COMPANIONS, and I AM their Shaykh and Trainer."

I have personally seen terrible things that happened to people who left this Ahmadi-Muhammadi-Ibrahimi-Tijani Way out of disrespect, apathy or laziness. Some left Islam entirely, some got on drugs, became afflicted with evil jinn, enslaved themselves to the dunya, lost their wealth and many such things. What awaits in the Hereafter maybe worse. One may play with everything, except Allah (swt) and His Prophet (saws). al-Shaykh al-Tijani (ra) will either make you or break you.

The Prophet (saws) even guaranteed Jannah to those who just love al-Khatm al-Awliya' al-Shaykh Ahmad al-Tijani (ra), even without taking the Wird and even if they are sinners. He (saws) said to him (ra) openly, "You are from the Safe ones, and all those who love you will be saved. You are the door of Salvation for every sinner that attaches himself to you." By Allah (swt), be sincere to him (ra) and you will gain the Best in Both Worlds.

May Allah (swt) keep us steadfast on this Ahmadi- Muhammadi-Ibrahimi-Tijani Way, and forgive all our shortcomings. Amin.

Q: Is the existence of a communal center [*Zawiya*; pl. *zawaya*] in every community of Tijaniyyin obligatory or optional? What is the urgency and significance of being a *Zawiya* for a Tijani congregation? What is the difference between performing one's *Tijaniyya* in a masjid, house or other places and in *Zawiya*?

A: It is strongly encouraged for every large Tijani community to build a Zawiya where they can come together to recite the adhkar of the Tariqa. Otherwise, they will be forced to perform the adhkar in a masjid or someone's house, both of which may be inconvenient for people. To make adhkar like the Wazifa and the Dhikr al-Jumu'a in congregation is necessary. If nobody in your town is making them in congregation, then all Tijaniyyin in your town will be guilty of a major sin (in Tariqa). Any muqaddam must make sure they bring the brothers and sisters together as much as they can, at least once a week for the Dhikr al-Jumu'a. Note also that a Zawiya should only be built with the permission of our shuyukh.

Shaykh Sidi Ahmad al-Tijani (ra) built the Zawiya al-Kubra in Fez, Morocco, in the year 1800 CE, with direct permission and instruction from the blessed Prophet (saws); who also guaranteed to him that every Salah performed in his Zawiya will be accepted by Allah (swt) for sure.

When the Sultan of Morocco wanted to donate money for building the Zawiya, the Shaykh (ra) refused saying:

زاويتنا أمرها قائم بالله

"*The affairs of our Zawiya are taken care of by Allah (swt).*"

The Shaykh (ra) also said about his Zawiya:

"*If the greatest Gnostics knew what is concealed in my Zawiya from Divine Blessings, they would camp there forever.*"

Indeed, after the building of the Zawiya al-Kubra, the Shaykh (ra) was ordered by the Prophet (saws) to bury the special Greatest Name of Allah (ism al-'azam) in it. This was the Shaykh's special

Zawiya of Fez and first official center of the Tariqa.

However, the first Tijani Zawiya to be built in history was in the Algerian village of Guemar in 1789 CE, by some Muqaddamun of the Shaykh (ra) with his permission.

Throughout history, Tijani zawaya have been centers of learning and knowledge, dhikr, jihad (greater and lesser), and service to mankind. Zawaya require great respect as well, as the Prophet (saws) and the Shaykh (ra) are present in them always. Any service [*khidma*] for our zawaya is a great investment in this world and the Hereafter.

The lines written on the Door of the Zawiya al-Kubra say it all:

> *The Zawiyahs of the honorable Tijani*
> *Are established by the permission of the Best of Creation!*
> *And they are meant for those who wish to praise Allah*
> *And send Salawat upon the Prophet (SAW) with sincerity!*

Q: Why must we follow the Sunna and ahadith? Is not the Qur'an enough? I have heard that the ahadith were not even preserved and most of them are made-up.

A: The Blessed Qur'an commands us in numerous Verses to "obey the Prophet (saws)", "Take what he (saws) gives you", "Avoid what he (saws) forbids you", "He (saws) is the best example for you"… all in addition to the original order of "Obey Allah." Allah would not have ordered us to obey the Prophet (saws) if the teachings of the Prophet (saws) were not to be preserved and known.

The first Muslims, the Sahaba (ra), took the above Divine Commandments seriously, and therefore obeyed the Prophet (saws) in everything and noted all his teachings and counsels (which then became known as "al-Sunna"). Then it was these same Sahaba who passed down both the Qur'an and the Sunna to future generations, as the sources of Islam.

By claiming now to follow "only the Qur'an", one is basically saying:

- "I disobey those Verses of the Qur'an which order me to obey the Prophet (saws) and take him as an example" (how can I if nothing of his teachings is preserved anyways?)

- "I will take from the Prophet (saws) the Qur'an only, but I will not take anything else from him"

- "I will trust the Sahaba to deliver the Qur'an to me but I don't trust them to deliver the Sunna!"

Needless to say, such an attitude does not make any sense. By rejecting the Sunna, one must categorically reject the Qur'an as well, as they both come to us from the same sources: The Prophet (saws) and the Sahaba. Therefore, by rejecting the Sunna, we are destroying the foundations of Islam itself.

Furthermore, the Prophetic Sunna is there to explain the Qur'an, as the Qur'an itself states (check for example the initial Verses of Surah al-Jumu'a [62]). Allah states that He has sent us the Book and its Teacher (saws). So are we going to say to Allah: We accept the Book but we don't accept the Teacher (saws)?

Indeed, without the Sunna, many injunctions of the Qur'an would be impossible to fulfill. For example, the Qur'an orders us to establish prayer,

Frequently Asked Questions (Faqs)

but nowhere does it explain how the prayer is done. This is only learned from the ahadith. Without the ahadith, we will also not be able to know the various backgrounds [asbab al-nuzul] of the various suras of the Qur'an, as well as their merits, number of verses, etc. In short, the Qur'an cannot be practiced without the Sunna.

Of course, I understand that throughout the years, many fabrications crept into the large corpus of the ahadith. However, our great scholars (ra) have worked hard to weed these out and set methodologies for us also to weed them out. It is very easy to know which of the Sunna is very authentic, which is semi-authentic, which is questionable, and what is fabrication. We should not throw the baby out with the bath water.

The Sunna is full of great Prophetic Treasures. I will advise people to study it before they judge it. A good start would be the <u>40 Ahadith (al-Arba'in)</u> of Imam al-Nawawi (ra), and <u>Riyad al-Salihin</u> by him, as well. It would be a lie and a shame for us Muslims to claim that the Ummah preserved the Word of Allah, the Qur'an, but did not preserve anything from the Words of his Final Prophet (saws)!

Q: I recall a statement wherein Shaykh Ibrahim Niasse said that some people may be among the Awliya', but they were not necessarily 'Arifin, and that such is possible as indicated in the Jawahir al-Rasa'il. How this is possible?

A: As for some pious people being Awliya' (friends of Allah) and not 'Arifin (knowers of Allah), this is quite possible as complete gnosis [Ma'rifa], an indicator of the maqam of Ihsan, is not a necessity for sainthood [walaya].

Walaya means becoming the Beloved of Allah, and this can happen to someone who is not an 'arif, also. What is required for walaya though is perfection in the spiritual stations before Ihsan (e.g. Islam and Iman).

There are men and women who have such strong Iman, that their consciousness of Allah's Overwhelming Presence is nearly the same as the 'Arifin, who actually witness this Presence and not just believe in it. Such strong Iman is called the beginning of true gnosis [*ma'rifa al-sughra*]. So these people may be Awliya' but not 'Arifin.

Indeed, we have seen many like that, especially outside of the Fayda Tijaniyya. They are beloved people [*ahbab*] of Allah (swt), but not Knowers of the Absolute Reality [*Haqiqa*].

The 'Arifin are higher in rank and more beloved to Allah. If it were not like that, Allah (swt) would not have revealed His Absolute Secret to them. In short, every 'arif is a Wali, but not every Wali is an 'arif.

Shaykh Ibrahim (ra) called the first category "the Awliya' of the Shari'a" and the second category "the Awliya' of the Haqiqa."

Of course, the 'Arifin remain Beloveds of Allah (swt) so far as they are engaged in the service of Allah and devotion to Him. Once they cease doing that and actively engages in sin and disobedience, then the Ma'rifa will "fly away from their heart" as Shaykh Ibrahim said. Then he will lose Ma'rifa, walaya and everything. May Allah protect us, bi-jahi al-Habib (saws). Amin.

Q: What is the purpose of hadiya, and what is the adab in giving/receiving it?

A: Hadiya means gift. A gift is given to display our love, respect or appreciation, or all of the above.

The Sahaba, may Allah be pleased with them all, used to give gifts to the Prophet (saws), who himself said: "Give gifts to each other, it will increase your love [tahada'u tahabbu]," and would accept them.

There is much blessing in giving gifts to one's shaykh or muqaddam, even if they do not need it… and more so if they do! It purifies one's heart and increases the provision and wealth.

Many of our shuyukh have dedicated their entire lives to the work of the Din and the Tariqa. These gifts, mostly monetary in nature, help them host their many guests and provide for the many poor people who come to them for assistance.

However, a real Wali relies only on Allah , and never on the gifts of his Murideen. While he accepts the hadiya, he does not seek it. His heart is not at all attached to the wealth of the aspirant(s). Sayyidina Shaykh Ahmad al-Tijani, may Allah sanctify his Secret, strictly warned the Muqaddamun to "not to be greedy for what is in the hands of your disciples. Be needy of Allah only."

Therefore, it is unacceptable for a muqaddam to demand a hadiya. Many such demanders are spiritual fraudsters who are selling the Din for the dunya.

My advice: Give hadaya to those who don't ask for it. Beware of those who do ask!

Glossary

Adab: manners, ethics

Akhira: afterlife, hereafter

Aqtab: saintly poles (plural of **Qutb**)

'Arifin: people with gnosis (plural of **'arif**)

Awliya': friends of Allah (plural of **Wali**)

Bay'a: to take an oath of allegiance or commitment

Dhikr: remembrance of Allah

Du'a: supplication

Dunya: the world, present life

Fat'h: spiritual opening

Ghusl: full-body ablution (bath, shower)

Hadith: recorded sayings and actions of the Prophet (asws)

Hafiz: a scholar who has memorized the entire *Qur'an* and/or at least 100,000 *ahadith* and their meanings

'Ibada: acts of worship

Ihsan: third level of the Din, perfection of worship

Iman: second level of the Din, absolute belief and certainty

Insha'llah: "if Allah wills"

Istighfar: the act of seeking Allah's forgiveness

Kashf: spiritual unveiling, seeing the unseen with the permission of Allah

Ma'rifa: experienced knowledge (gnosis) of Allah **Muqaddam:** authorized representative of the Tariqa

Murideen: aspirants (plural of **Murid**)

The divine opening

Qibla: direction of Muslims prayer (Mecca)

Qiyamah: The Day of Rising

Qutb: saintly pole (the highest position of gnosis)

(RA): abbrev. "May Allah be pleased with such person(s) (radiya'llahu 'anhu/'anha/'anhum)

Sahaba: a companion of the Prophet Muhammad (asws)

Salah : ritual prayer of a Muslim

Salawat: plural, salutations of peace and blessings upon the Prophet (e.g. 'alayhi Salatu wa salam, salla'llahu 'alayhi wa sallim)

Shari'a: sacred law of *Islam*

Sunna: traditions and approved actions of the Prophet (asws)

Tahara: purity

Tahlil: the phrase "la ilaha illa Allah"

Tasawwuf: Sufism, the science of the Murid seeking perfection of worship

Tawhid: divine Oneness of Allah

Tayammum: dry ablution with dust, sand, rock

Tarbiya: spiritual training for the attainment of gnosis

Tariqa: spiritual path

Tazkiya: purification, the method of the Murid seeking perfection of worship

Turuq: paths (plural of **Tariqa**)

'Ulama': *Islamic* scholars (plural of **'alim**)

Wali: saint, friend of Allah

Wasiyya: advice, counsel

Wazifa: lit. "office", congregational remembrance of the Tariqa Tijaniyya

Wird: litany, select combinations of Names of Allah and ayat of *Qur'an* which are recited consistently

Wudu': partial-body ablution

Zawiya: lit. "lodge", place of gathering for congregational *dhikr*

Zakah: a pillar of *Islam*, 2.5% of annual wealth given to poor and indigent

www.ingramcontent.com/pod-product-compliance
Lightning Source LLC
Chambersburg PA
CBHW050543300426
44113CB00012B/2237